P9-DZX-875

OPEN YOUR HEART

with Gardens

*"*You have hit the mark on my favorite topic: using gardening to open the heart and mind to everything positive. When my own life was changing, and my outlook needed overhauling, I went to the garden. Everything good began to happen after that. And as I look back on the last twenty years, I see where I actually let my personal door open to allow my good life to come in.*"*

—Patricia Lanza, creator of the Lasagna Gardening system, and author of *Lasagna Gardening, Lasagna Gardening for Small Spaces,* and *Lasagna Gardening with Herbs*

❁

*"*This heartwarming book explains not only how to garden, but why we garden. A good read especially suitable for family gardening.*"*

—Mel Bartholomew, originator and author of the *All New Square Foot Gardening* book and method, and author of the largest selling garden book in America, EVER

❁

*"*Full of great, versatile ideas and info. A wonderful potpourri for anyone interested in gardening, whether a beginner or professional.*"*

—Nancy Rowe, Master Gardener

*"*An inspirational primer for gardeners who want to cultivate herbs, vegetables, or fruit trees, and cook simple, whole foods for their families—like our mothers and grandmothers did.*"*

—Barbara Ghazarian, author of *Simply Armenian: Naturally Healthy Ethnic Cooking Made Easy*

*"*In the spare time I don't have I continue to read your garden book. It really is great. It's GREAT. WOW. I just love it. I'm so inspired. That was the purpose, right?*"*

—Leslie Noyes, Designer, Leslie Noyes Creative Consulting

Praise for the
OPEN YOUR HEART series

*"*It's a great idea!*"*

—Regis Philbin

*"*The OPEN YOUR HEART series is a winning combination that both instructs and inspires.*"*

—Hazel Dixon-Cooper, author of *Born On a Rotten Day* and *Love On a Rotten Day,* and *Cosmopolitan Magazine*'s Bedside Astrologer

*"*The perfect books to improve your mind, get in shape, and find inspiration.*"*

—Bonnie Hearn Hill, author of *Intern, Killer Body,* and the Geri LaRue newspaper thriller series

OPEN YOUR HEART

with
Gardens

Mastering Life through Love of Plants

CAROLYN HALEY

DreamTime Publishing, Inc.

DreamTime Publishing, Inc., books are available at special quantity discounts for bulk purchases for sales promotions, premiums, fund-raising, and educational needs. Please contact us at www.DreamTimePublishing.com for additional information.

Library of Congress Cataloging-in-Publication Data

Haley, Carolyn.
　　Open your heart with gardens : mastering life through love of plants / Carolyn Haley.— 1st ed.
　　　p. cm.
　　Includes index.
　　ISBN-13: 978-1-60166-012-1 (trade pbk.)
　　1. Gardening—Anecdotes. 2. Gardens—Anecdotes. 3. Gardeners—Anecdotes. 4. Haley, Carolyn. I. Title.
　　SB455.H322 2008
　　635—dc22
　　　　　　　　　　　　　　　　　　　　　　　　　　2007041535

Branding, website, and cover design for DreamTime Publishing by
　　Rearden Killion • www.reardenkillion.com
Illustrations by Janice Marie Phelps • www.janicephelps.com
Manuscript consulting by Jeannette Cézanne • www.customline.com
Helen McDonald, final line editing • hmproofreading@msn.com
Text layout and design by Gary A. Rosenberg • www.garyarosenberg.com

This publication is designed to provide accurate and authoritative information in regard to the subject matter covered. It is sold with the understanding that the publisher is not engaged in rendering legal, accounting, or other professional service. If legal advice or other expert assistance is required, the services of a competent professional person should be sought.

　　—From a declaration of principles jointly adopted by a committee of the American Bar Association and a committee of publishers.

This book is printed on recycled, acid-free paper containing a minimum of 50% recycled, de-inked fiber.

Contents

We may have to learn again the
mystery of the garden: how its external
characteristics model the heart itself,
and how the soul is a garden enclosed,
our own perpetual paradise where
we can be refreshed and restored.

—THOMAS MOORE,
THE RE-ENCHANTMENT OF EVERYDAY LIFE

Note from the Publisher

Balancing the overall mission of a series of books with each author's individual creativity and vision is an enjoyable and rewarding challenge. The goal of this note is to tie the loose ends together to make your experience with this book as meaningful as possible.

We have two goals with the Open Your Heart series. The first is to provide you with practical advice about your hobby or interest, in this case gardens. We trust this advice will increase your ongoing enjoyment of gardens or even encourage you to explore a new activity.

Our second goal is to help you use what you know and love to make the rest of your life happier and easier. This process worked in different ways for each of our writers, so it will likely work in different ways for each of you. For some, it's a matter of becoming more self-aware. Just realizing what makes you happy while enjoying the fresh air and working with the earth—or enjoying others' work with the earth—and then gradually learning to use those feelings as a barometer when dealing with your job, relationships, and other issues could be an important first step. For others, gardens provide an important outlet for stress and contemplation, allowing you to go back into your daily life refreshed. For yet others, you might discover how to meditate, how to connect with the mysterious flow of the Universe when you are immersed in Nature. Once you recognize the beauty of that for what it is, you can then learn to connect with the flow in other ways at other times.

We are not suggesting you will find all of your answers in this book. We are, though, inviting you to look at something you love with new eyes, a new perspective, and a new heart. Once you recognize the importance of feeling good in one area of your life, you are open to feeling good in the rest of your life. And that is the cornerstone to mastering your life.

Happy reading!

Meg Bertini

Meg Bertini
Publisher

Acknowledgments

Many thanks to Leslie and Cynthia of the Green Mountain Goddesses writing circle, along with satellite members Barbara and Caroline, for their ideas and support. Also to my editor, Jeannette, whose guidance and cheerleading helped put it all together, and to my spouse, Charlie, for being a rock.

Extra-special thanks to all the contributors who shared their souls, showing us all how to open our hearts to gardens.

Introduction

Some people grumble because roses have thorns;
I am thankful that the thorns have roses.

—ALPHONSE KARR

*E*ach year, it happens afresh:

After months of brown and gray and white . . . cold and hard and dark . . . the day comes when I step outside and behold a tip of green protruding from the ground.

The first daffodil!

The sight of it drops me to my knees, mentally chanting, *Thankyouthankyouthankyou!* Then I leap up into The Happy Dance because there at my feet lies proof that the world has kept turning, the invisible forces of the universe have kept churning, and Mother Nature has again fulfilled her promise despite everything I doubted and feared.

Thankyouthankyouthankyou!

People who live in dry climates probably feel this way when the rains come, as do folks in gray and soggy places when the sun finally emerges. Me, I live in the mountains of northern New

England, where snow can be on the ground from October through May, and every winter, for days—sometimes weeks—the temperatures can sit at double-digits below zero. The environment becomes a cruel antagonist. I can't imagine how anything, much less a tender plant, survives.

To me it's a miracle when that first daffodil breaks through. The annual surge of joy and gratitude that accompanies it is what first opened my heart to gardens.

It started, indeed, with daffodils. Inspired by their signal of spring rebirth, and cheered into summer by their happy yellow, I needed to ensure they came back; so I planted more in autumn. Hope for their survival carried me through winter. They rewarded me the following spring, year after year after year.

Like sunshine incarnate, daffodils warmed my soul enough to want to share the glow with other people. I began planting bulbs every autumn wherever I lived, whether the landlord allowed gardens or not. Many times I changed dwellings so soon that I never saw whether the daffodils grew and blossomed. Knowing that they probably did—and that I'd left behind a ray of sunshine—let me move on without regret into the next chapter of my life.

Eventually I came to rest at a home I could call my own, complete with somebody else's left-behind garden: overgrown, in some places hidden, a relic of love begging to be revived. We moved in during the depth of winter, so that first spring was a bounty of discovery. And that first autumn I planted daffodil bulbs. The following spring, some of them blossomed. Ironically, here at my permanent residence, many of my daffodils have failed to return in subsequent years. Trying to figure out why, and how to build the swath of them I've always dreamed of, pulled me into the mysteries of plant lore—doubly provoked by the daffodil clusters planted by the previous owner, which thrive in the shady bog where they're not supposed to be able to grow.

I never consciously decided to garden. Instead, my heart was captured by something elemental that led to a richness of experience I didn't imagine yet sought in other places but never found.

I guess I was predisposed to it, given that our suburban family home was the only one on the street without a rectangular, uniformly green front lawn. Instead, it was edged with a low stone wall containing a solid mass of myrtle, through which flagstones zigzagged to the front door. A Japanese maple arched as centerpiece, and random sparks of yellow, white, and purple crocus popped up each spring. Toward the end of the season, a flowering quince dropped gold orbs into the underbrush, while a wisteria that canopied the front porch dropped long, crunchy pods. Midsummer, we competed with the birds for blueberries in the backyard, and ate tomatoes that didn't come from the store. All because my mother had opened her heart to gardens.

She's the one who gave me the poetry book that inclined my own heart to daffodils. I was nine, and it was a winter gift— "Happy New Year," she inscribed—one of the first books of my own. Amid its delightful and poignant mix of verses was this classic:

I Wandered Lonely as a Cloud

William Wordsworth
(from *Poems in Two Volumes*, 1807)

I wandered lonely as a cloud
That floats on high o'er vales and hills,
When all at once I saw a crowd—
A host, of golden daffodils,
Beside the lake, beneath the trees,
Fluttering and dancing in the breeze.

Continuous as the stars that shine
And twinkle on the Milky Way,
They stretched in never-ending line
Along the margin of a bay;
Ten thousand saw I, at a glance,
Tossing their heads in sprightly dance.

The waves beside them danced, but they
Out-did the sparkling waves in glee;
A poet could not but be gay
In such a jocund company;
I gazed and gazed—but little thought
What wealth the show to me had brought.

For oft, when on my couch I lie,
In vacant or in pensive mood,
They flash upon that inward eye
Which is the bliss of solitude,
And then my heart with pleasure fills,
And dances with the daffodils.

In the decades since, I've found that while the sunrise gets me
through each day, the daffodils get me through each year.

—Carolyn

ONE

A Primer of Possibilities

A garden is like life: something is always doing well,
something is struggling, something is being born anew,
and something is dying.

—EDITH REED

*E*eny, meeny, miny, moe—how many ways can I make my garden grow?

There are so many options that finding the right one for you may seem daunting. Happily, the diversity of these options guarantees that the right one for you lies among them.

Sometimes circumstances make the choice for you. At our place, the lay of the land has forced me to try different approaches, many of which I'll share with you in this book. Now I manage a combination of garden setups and conduct new experiments every year.

What helps is the flexibility inherent—nay, required—in gardening. Indeed, gardening is perhaps the most flexible and individualistic of pastimes. No two pockets of soil are the same, no two plants of the same species will bear identical fruit or flowers, no day's weather will match any other's. Add in your own variables—time, resources, temperament, health—and you're guaranteed that whatever you undertake will always be uniquely your own.

This opens the door to a personalized experience unavailable in other activities. Especially since your gardening partner is Nature—a capricious, opportunistic, and amoral force that can flick you off the planet without concern. We can't master Nature, only work in harmony with her. And that harmony brings a sense of achievement; of peace; of humility and purpose and place that can only be known in a garden.

(Mountain climbers might argue that last sentence, since they can experience the same feelings at a summit. However, I believe that the top of Mount Everest belongs to "God's Garden"— which comprises all of the great outdoors—so the statement holds true.)

Any garden gives respite from the travails of daily existence. Gardens almost force you to open your heart, since any act involving them requires a mental gear change that engages you in the moment and automatically relaxes your mind. Suddenly you're dealing with elementals: earth, air, water, color, aroma. A nonstop drama involving birth and growth and death, on a timescale unrelated to human concerns.

Plants are so different from us that they might as well be Martians. Yet, they are alive, and need the same basics we do in order to thrive. The rules of engagement are therefore the same, yet different. That puts us off balance in a stimulating way.

We can't communicate with plants as we can with people and animals, so we must switch modes of thinking in order to interact with plants. They pull our attention outward, making it impossible to concentrate on personal problems. Enter a garden and presto!—there goes worry, and aches and pains, and hurt and pride and anger. Losing these relaxes the mind, creating the necessary first step to emotional ease and rational focus, which in turn are what we need in order to master our lives.

Gardens can be interacted with on so many levels that everyone can experience something positive from them, be it a moment of delight from a glimpse of beauty, or a memory conjured by a whiff of fragrance—all the way to the grandest scale, where one can experience awe and wonder bordering on rapture, and a lifetime of satisfying work.

You might, like me, balk at my use of the word "everyone." We all know people and lifestyles that are utterly and forever incompatible with plants. No argument here—no statement ever applies to *everyone*. But therein lies the point. Everyone is different. Everyone's life goes through phases. The same is true for gardens, which allow everyone access to them on individual terms.

A Garden

A garden is filled with peace.
A garden may bring to stress a healthy release.
A garden may be filled with flowers, fragrant and sweet.
A garden may be filled with the best of food to eat.
A garden may be mixtures of green
or green plants with a cast of silver sheen.
A garden may be of flowers white
that shine and glow in the evening light.
A garden may be of shades of pink,
a good place to sit and think.
A garden may be of blossoms red,
the showiest of all the flowers in the bed.
A garden may be of flowers blue,
a restful place when the day is through.
A garden may have gold and yellows
that blend their hues with their bed fellows.

A garden may be all colors of the rainbow,
a place where Hummingbird and Butterfly put on their
   ballet show.
A garden requires time to spend.
A garden is a wonderful place to share with a friend.
A garden can be a place to sip a cup of tea.
A garden is a place for you and me.

Eunice Lehman / Versailles, Missouri

The average person, upon hearing the term "garden," may think of a green space filled with flowers and vegetables. My dictionary includes other definitions:

❀ A plot of ground where herbs, fruits, flowers, or vegetables are cultivated.

❀ A rich well-cultivated region.

❀ A container (such as a window box) housing a variety of small plants.

❀ A public recreation area or park usually ornamented with plants and trees.

❀ An open-air eating or drinking place.

❀ A large hall for public entertainment.

For me, "garden" means all of the above. For you, it's whatever way you choose to capture the spirit of the living green world. Many people relish getting their hands dirty, using direct approaches outlined in the next three chapters. Subsequent chapters offer ways to enjoy gardens without lifting a finger.

TWO

In the Dooryard— General Gardening Systems

The greatest gift of the garden
is the restoration of the five senses.

—HANNA RION

When I moved to Vermont, I learned a new word: dooryard. This describes the main area of activity around a home, outside the doors—front, back, side—which is where, when you think about it, most of us spend our outdoor time.

Although originally a rural New England term, I've extended it to include suburban and urban patios, porches, terraces, front stoops, balconies, decks, and carports . . . all those places where we step outside and interact with the world without actually going anywhere; the places where most of us install our gardens.

Traditional Gardening

Dig hole in dirt, insert plant, cover, and water. Unless you have truly terrible soil, and/or a run of really bad weather, you will almost always get a return for your efforts. That's how I started: plunking daffodil bulbs straight into the ground with no preparation or follow-up. This is sort of like teaching someone to swim by throwing them into the pool. The hardiest survive, but they can experience trauma and may not endure. I did indeed get daffodils from this practice, but never the dense bed I desired, and rarely did the same plants keep blooming for years.

Conversely, plants I have deliberately put into dubious corners have thrived, seeming to thumb their petals at me. Regardless, a dirt garden is what most people have available as an option. If properly cultivated, it can produce reliably and lushly for our lifespan and beyond.

There are two schools of thought on conventional dirt gardening: (1) give plants lots of room and keep them carefully mulched and weeded, so they can grow to maximum size without competing with anything, and stay well-ventilated to prevent disease; or (2) pack 'em in as tight as they'll grow without constriction, so that their foliage will shade the ground and smother out weeds, as well as hold in moisture, and they will yield heartily.

Choosing which system to use depends on available space as much as it does on philosophy. It also depends on the fitness of one's body or wallet: digging takes muscle or horsepower as well as time. Once done, however, inground beds are easy to sustain, for all you have to do to keep them nourished is add compost. And they allow closer contact with Nature than other systems provide.

All garden setups require maintenance and cleanup according to the season. Therefore, the decision to develop an outdoor soil garden versus any other type revolves around your inclinations and lifestyle.

When the time comes that creativity falters, energy diminishes, and living conditions change, the joys of being outdoors and around gardens can continue, if not actually increase. The emphasis changes from creating and cultivating to maintaining and neatening.

When one's own garden is reduced to a condominium mini-garden, the pure pleasure of just being outside and seeing the beauty of nature and gardens enhanced by one's ability to pull weeds, trim and prune, albeit it in another's garden, can be as satisfying and rewarding as creating and working in one's own.

So, when my busy children see Mother's little car drive up, they know there are gardening gloves, hand clippers, and bug repellant in the backseat and she is here to do what they call *work* and she calls *play*!

Marjorie K. Haley / Unionville, Connecticut

Lasagna Gardening

Don't want to dig? Try a lasagna garden! Although labor-intensive to set up the first time, this labor does not compare to digging and tilling. Instead, a lasagna garden starts on top of the ground and is built up just like the casserole it's named for: a layer of this, a layer of that, a layer of this, then topping.

Essentially, lasagna gardening is sheet composting. It was formalized into an approach for home gardeners by Patricia Lanza, who has published three books on the subject: *Lasagna Gardening*, *Lasagna Gardening for Small Spaces*, and *Lasagna Gardening with Herbs*. It's a dream solution for people unwilling or unable to dig, and/or where the soil is inadequate or downright hostile. All you do is lay down a base (wet newspapers, for example), then scrounge or buy natural materials to layer on top of it (peat moss, compost, brush or grass trimmings, topsoil, leaves, etc.). Then pull open a hole in the top layer and put in your plants. Coat the garden surface with whatever form of mulch is available, and add new layer(s) each year. Other than watering, your only task is to weed, if desired, then harvest.

When I tried to plant a flower in the yard of my new—my first—home, I quickly discovered why the previous owners hadn't put in any gardens. It was almost impossible to dig through the combination of brick-hard clay soil and rocks. I despaired of ever making my visions of lush, colorful gardens a reality. Then my friend loaned me a book about lasagna gardens. Upon reading the book, I realized I already had most of the recommended materials (newspaper, composted dirt, and old leaves). After a quick trip to the garden store for peat moss I had everything I needed.

My sister and I installed beds along the side of my house in one afternoon. It was by far the easiest garden bed preparation either of us had ever done. No need to tear up the sod. No digging to break up the soil. In fact, nothing that two (not entirely young) women couldn't handle all on our own.

Everything I plant in the lasagna garden flourishes. The spongy soil retains water through dry summer days, and adding plants is a snap. Next season I plan to put another lasagna garden on top of a pile of building rubble the previous owners left in the yard, and then one for veggies. In fact, I see no reason to use any other method to prepare new beds!

Lasagna gardens are an ideal option for first-time gardeners, people who can't physically tackle rototillers or hand-turning soil, and those among us who aren't blessed with rich, easy-to-work soil.

Laurie Fila /
Germantown, New York

Lasagna Garden

I haven't yet run a cycle of seasons with my own lasagna garden; I've only just built it, and am letting the layers settle over the winter. This will allow instant planting in the spring. When I first learned about lasagna gardens, I fell in love with the idea and spent the next two years accumulating the yard waste and base materials needed to make one. That left just peat moss to buy. Good thing that's all I had to buy, for the little bed (10 feet long, 4 feet wide, 9 inches deep) consumed three big, compressed bales (3.8 cubic feet each) of peat moss plus all the materials I had compiled, and then some. For ladies constructing lasagna beds on their own, note that this size of peat moss cube is very awkward and heavy.

That was the hardest part of the project. Everything else I could lift on my own power or trundle around with a wheelbarrow. It took a whole day of short, widely spaced work sessions to construct the bed. But it was easy work, undertaken on one of those days when having any excuse to be outdoors is a blessing. The pleasure was amplified by the excitement of starting something new—all my gardens for the past decade have been revivals of existing beds, or containers. The lasagna system promises low-labor abundance while giving me a clean slate on which to design my dream layout. Winter will fly by this year as I lose myself in fantasy, sketching out plans for next spring.

Container Gardening

When I started gardening, I used the traditional method, digging in the backyard in an area established by the previous homeowner. My techniques ranged from winging it to meticulously employing the square-foot technique discussed below. Ultimately I transferred those efforts to EarthBoxes on my deck.

An EarthBox is self-watering planter designed to be an all-in-one garden unit. You can purchase kits with instructions from the originator or follow the concept with a homemade version. An EarthBox comprises a rectangular bucket large enough to grow multiple plants of any kind—including corn and tomatoes—with a reservoir in the bottom accessed by a watering tube in a top corner.

You fill the container with water, then add potting soil, which rests above the water on a screen. Next, run a band of fertilizer across the soil surface, cover the container with mulch (the kit comes with an elasticized black fabric cover that can be reused) into which you cut holes to insert the plants. Water them via the tube every few days. You know the reservoir is full when water starts trickling out a hole in the side of the planter.

I started with one EarthBox and did a comparison test with peppers: six in the garden, six in the box. Come end of season, the garden yield was small and sparse, while the EarthBox gave me a full crop of big, tasty bells. The next year—because I favor red peppers over green ones—I moved the containers inside when frost arrived and harvested red peppers until Christmas in my living room. (Not a wise practice, however, for a host of mites came indoors with them, and I dribbled dirt-stained water all over the carpet!) EarthBoxes, when full, cannot be picked up by an ordinary human being.

Box success moved me to do all my gardening in containers. Someday I hope to combine this practice with season extenders and indoor growing. For the short term, I've found these pluses to container gardening: flexibility of location, control of the environment, and improved yield. The minuses: what to do with the containers in winter, keeping the soil good, and moving them around (also, practicing crop rotation).

Converting to containers is initially expensive. And unless you mix your own soil (a hefty out-of-pocket expense when you first buy the ingredients), you must purchase cubic yards of potting soil in heavy bags.

This isn't true if you're only doing a window box or a few small pots on a railing. For setting up a garden that will feed you, or surround you with blossoms, you need lots of pots and a whole bunch of soil. But container gardening suits many people's preferences and settings. It allows gardens to be placed where no ground space is available and to move them inside, or to have doorstep access to special plants with a main garden farther away in a yard.

Every spring for the past three or four years I have had container gardens and small flowerbeds. I've grown pansies, peony roses, crocuses, daffodils, vinca vines, and a variety of herbs. I love to cook, so having fresh herbs on my doorstep is a thrill. All summer long I water them, watch for pests, and snip a little here and there for my nightly salad, to put into bread dough, or to use in marinades. (My boyfriend laughs at me when I thank the plants out loud each time I snip a leaf or a twig. But I figure the plant is a living thing giving up part of itself to sustain me, so the least I can do is say thanks!) I've grown chives, rosemary, cilantro, parsley, thyme, purple basil, sweet basil, and oregano.

Having fresh herbs to cook with makes me feel like I am part of a female tradition going back centuries. When I use the basil I imagine Italian women using it, when I smell the oregano I dream up all sorts of wonderful Greek recipes. The herbs are beautiful to look at, smell heavenly, and seem to unlock my inner desire to cook a wonderful meal that is as close to the land as possible. I try to use local vegetables, fruits, and berries with my herbs. For a while I lived in an area where I could pick wild onions from my backyard!

I grew up in a very large family where we grew nearly all our own vegetables, and, despite long nights spent weeding in a cloud of black flies I guess some of my father's love of the land rubbed off on me. I think Dad gardened mainly because he grew up during the Depression (he was born in 1928). To him it seemed wasteful to buy a carrot or a potato when you could grow one. Our root cellar was always full of potatoes and turnips slowly shriveling in the dark, extending creepy "eyes" up out of the bins. I remember drying onions on wool blankets on the lawn.

As an extension of the gardening, my mom would make pickles, pickled beets (yum!), and tomato chowchow. The apple trees in my grandparents' orchard next door yielded apple butter and crab apple jelly. All summer long we picked all kinds of wild berries on our property (blueberries, blackberries, wild strawberries, and raspberries), and tiny sweet tree fruit that we called "wild pears" but I think were actually a kind of berry. Eventually Dad planted strawberry plants and we got larger berries, but they were nothing like the wild ones that grew on the lawn!

I often think of my family when I'm weeding the flower beds, and it turns a tedious chore into a peaceful pastime.

Kelly Smith / Coloma, Michigan

Square Foot Gardening

One of the neatest, most compact, and efficient systems for gardening is the square-foot method developed by Mel Bartholomew. It breaks the process into manageable, easy-to-understand steps based on squares instead of rows. This system gave me the mental and physical tools I needed to successfully implement a vegetable garden. I found it not only easy but fun—and fruitful!

The square-foot principles and techniques are so versatile they can be applied to any other system, such as lasagna gardening or container gardening. They suit beginning and experienced gardeners alike and guarantee great results.

This has been proven by the book's success: the original *Square Foot Gardening* became the largest-selling garden book in America and led to a TV show that ran on PBS for five years, followed by the Discovery network and The Learning Channel (TLC) for another three years. The follow-up book, *CASH from Square Foot Gardening,* shows anyone how to earn up to $15,000 in their backyard every year! A related book, *A Teacher's Lesson Plan for Children,* has been used in many school systems.

Bartholomew's square-foot system has been converted to square-meter gardening and is now used all over the world. In 2007 he released an updated version: *All New Square Foot Gardening.*

After I retired from my engineering company, I took up gardening as a hobby, but became very disappointed. I tried the conventional single-row method everyone was doing back then, but there seemed to be so much work, so many weeds, and an overwhelming harvest all at once.

There also seemed to be a terrible waste of space, since the rows were supposed to be placed three feet apart, even though the plants were only three, six, or nine inches apart in the row. I couldn't understand why we were taught to pour out a whole packet of seeds in each row . . . and then have to come back to thin most of the seedlings out. That just didn't make any sense. Another thing: if we planted the entire row at once, wouldn't it all come to harvest at once? Great for the farmer, but not for the homeowner!

So I took my questions around the country, asking all the gardening experts why we are taught all those things. I got the same answer from Maine to California: "'Cause that's the way we've always done it." Right then and there I said, "I'm going to invent a new and better way to garden."

After experimenting for a year, I came up with the idea of reducing the size of the garden, eliminating the backbreaking work every spring and the constant weeding all summer. I concentrated the garden into a much smaller area, actually four-foot by four-foot planting blocks, which you walk around and reach into. This eliminated the need to dig up a huge area every spring trying to loosen and improve your existing soil, year after year after year.

That reduction allowed me to grow 100 percent of the harvest in only 20 percent of the space. Now you could locate your garden much closer to the house, so you could take better care of it and enjoy it more often. Another really big advantage was you could start with a perfect soil that had *no weed seeds.* Now you didn't need to care what your existing ground was like. Then I worked out a spacing system for planting that took very little work and no more wasting of seeds.

I named my new method Square Foot Gardening (SFG), and it turned out so simple and easy that it works anywhere, especially where someone has very poor soil. This system is like no other, because it not only starts out with perfect soil the first year, it also employs a simple spacing method. Many systems still use single or staggered rows, merely spaced closer together than the old-fashioned three feet. Read any seed packet and see.

Basically, you lay out your SFG above ground with any number of four-foot by four-foot boxes, spaced three feet apart. Boxes keep the growing soil in place and your garden doesn't end up with that messy look to it. Start by laying down a weed barrier or landscape cloth inside your boxes, which are only six or eight inches deep. Fill them with a perfect soil mix, place a one-foot by one-foot grid on top, and you're ready to start planting.

After experimenting with many ingredients, I found the perfect soil blend, which I call Mel's Mix. It consists of just three ingredients: one-third each by volume of peat moss, vermiculite, and blended compost, all available at your local garden center. You'll never change your soil and it will last forever.

The number of plants that fit into each square foot are one, four, nine, or sixteen, depending on the size of the mature plant. If you plant a different crop in each square foot, sometimes flowers, sometimes vegetables or herbs, you'll create an attractive garden with no weeds and no huge harvest all at once. As each individual crop is finished, add a handful of compost to that square foot and replant with a different crop. This gives you crop rotation, soil improvement, and a continual harvest of those things you really want.

All vine crops—like tomatoes, cucumbers, squash, even melons—can be grown vertically on an upright frame attached to the garden box. The vine crops produce more fruit per square foot than any other method by growing right up nylon netting, which is attached to the vertical frame. The plants get better sunlight and air and become much healthier than caged or sprawling plants on the ground.

SFG works for any age and works in any location or situation, including decks, rooftops, and patios. You can even attach a plywood bottom to each box and raise it up on an outdoor table. Now you have a wheelchair, sit-down, or stand-up garden. Try that with any other backyard system! When you move, you simply take your box apart, put your soil in plastic bags, and put everything on the moving van.

Looking back on my gardening career these past thirty years, I think fondly of my mother's influence on my life. She always encouraged me to do everything just a little better, and in life: "Do whatever you can, to create a better world."

Thanks, Mom.

Mel Bartholomew / Eden, Utah

THREE

Do Your Own Thing— Creative Alternatives

Earth laughs in flower.

—RALPH WALDO EMERSON

No deity has ever decreed "All Gardens Must Be Outside and In Your Personal Space." Kind of hard to plant in the dooryard if you don't have one! Thanks to the infinite variety and flexibility of plants, you can garden indoors or out, on your own land or someone else's, sampling from an options list that reflects human ingenuity.

In all forms of gardening, you can specialize. Most everyone has a favorite flower or food they like to focus on; for instance, setting aside a patch for a cutting garden, or growing nothing but roses, or striving for the ultimate zucchini. I grow only enough vegetables to feed myself and my spouse for one season, planting only the types we like, then put the rest of my energies into flowers. Of these, I favor easy keepers that produce mass color. Yet I must always have daffodils and morning glories, because their colors cause a pleasurable ache in my heart.

My techniques are driven by the landscape and climate as much as by personal preference. The three combined have made it clear that there's no one best way to approach cultivation; in fact, diversity works just as well in the garden as it does in one's investment portfolio. Diversity, indeed, is Nature's way.

Hay Bale Gardening

A few years ago, while researching a problem with tomatoes via the Internet, I happened upon a story by a woman in the Midwest who grew her tomatoes in hay bales. This struck me as a wonderful idea: Stick a tomato in a hay bale, water daily, and harvest muchly. As the bale decays over the summer, it feeds the plant. How simple, how elegant! I decided to try it at first chance.

Eventually I obtained some hay bales from my neighbors, who keep an animal rescue farm and had some dusty hay unsuitable for their horses—but perfect for me. I found a sunny spot to place them in, then visited the Internet again to see if there was anything more I could learn about the process that might guarantee success.

What I learned was the difference between "simple" and "easy."

Hay bale gardening is simple. People have been growing produce and flowers this way for ages. However, their advice contained so many must-do's that I almost chucked the project in dismay. I went back to the original article: Yes, the woman said that all she does is water them every day, and counts her harvest in bushels. Everyone else said that I must first soak the bales with a hose every day for a week to get the decomposition started. Then I must only use a certain kind of straw, not hay (with disagreement on what the "right" straw is). Then I must set the plants in a bed of compost, then cover the bales with mulch. Most important, hay bales are directional—and I must set them so that the open side faces up, which allows water to penetrate more easily.

Having never handled a hay bale before, I was flummoxed by this directional element. I flopped a bale over and over, stuck my fingertips into it, and still couldn't figure out which was the cross grain and which was the open grain. Finally picked one, set the bales back into place, wrapped them in chicken wire so they wouldn't disintegrate or allow critters to munch on them, and let Mother Nature rain on them for a month.

When planting time came, I discovered that I had chosen the wrong grain direction. I needed a hole saw to cut an opening for the plants! Lacking that, I hacked away with a trowel and a serrated knife until I'd shredded a slot big enough to insert the seedling's root-ball. I stuffed some compost into it, followed by the plant. I poured water over it and watched water run off the tightly packed surface.

Then I ran up to the house and opened a package of drip spikes I had bought over the winter. These are little perforated cones you stick into the ground next to the roots of your plant. The top opening fits a standard liter or two-liter soda bottle. Plugged together, you get a crude drip waterer. Clearly, I was going to need this tool if my vegetables were going to survive the summer!

In less than a week, which included heat and rain and chill, I had a fine crop of mushrooms coating the top of all three bales! But the tomato, peppers, and zucchini I had planted were still alive.

By the end of the summer, things had changed dramatically and illustrated just how variable gardening can be. The zucchini? I'd planted a pair from the same six-pack into one hay bale. One grew huge and pumped out enough perfect fruits to feed us for months, with extras for zucchini bread; the second grew to half the size and started many small zucchini fingers, of which a small percentage reached maturity (though each was perfect).

Tomatoes had similar results. I had planted just one in its own hay bale, with its sister a few feet away in a self-watering container. Both were the same early-season variety. The container plant stayed small and pale but put out the first fruits of all my tomatoes, each perfect. The hay bale plant exploded into a jungle chock-full of fruits that matured weeks later. The plants were so different that I wondered if the nursery had somehow mislabeled varieties.

It's the same with the peppers to a different degree. I had planted a pair from the same seedling pack into one hay bale, as I did the zucchini. Then I planted the remaining four peppers from the six-pack a few feet away in a self-watering container. The container plants grew tall and consistent until ravaged by an insect pest. The hay bale plants, though, stayed small and their output was later and meager but insect-free. As with the tomatoes and zucchinis, I treated everybody the same—watering between rains, once or twice adding a liquid fertilizer.

Why everything came out so differently I'll never know. But clearly the hay bale system works. I will try it again next year. And bet that the results will differ once again!

Hanging Planter Gardening

Another nifty idea I encountered in my researches is the Topsy Turvy Planter. This is a kit composed of a bucket with a collared hole on each end allowing insertion of one or two plants so that they grow out the bottom and you water through the top. The kit includes a hanger, though you must come up with something strong enough to hang it from. (Once filled with soil, the planter weighs a good thirty pounds even when the plant is just a seedling. Add at least ten more for a good vegetable crop.)

My husband rigged up a compound pulley system off the

back deck that works a treat, after my wrought-iron "shepherd's crook" (designed for bird feeders and light planters) bowed nearly in half and pulled itself right out of the ground. We had discussed making our own upside-down planters out of five-gallon pails (do-it-yourself instructions can be found online, see Resources), but when I located an original Topsy Turvy kit for under ten dollars, I went for that instead.

The promotional materials and illustrations all feature tomatoes, which is what I wanted it for. A suspended tomato plant requires no digging, weeding, caging, or staking. It stays clean and dry so is less prone to pest infestation and disease. It's a great solution for urban gardeners, some of whom take things a step further and make "salad bowl" pots—growing herbs and lettuce in the top of a planter and tomatoes out the bottom.

Because the tomato grows down to you, you don't have to bend or reach to harvest. The system isn't recommended for indeterminate-type tomatoes—the viney ones that grow and grow and grow, and weigh a ton—which are also the ones that produce big slicing tomatoes—but it works fine for determinate types that limit their growth, or any other vegetable or flower.

Regular hanging planters (which won't bend a shepherd's crook!) can also be employed for compact gardening. They come in self-watering varieties as well as regular-old pots in plastic, ceramic, or wood. I prefer the self-watering type, since all containers must be watered more often than inground gardens, and containers with reservoirs gain you a bit of time between. The self-watering market is still young, however, so doesn't yet offer a great variety of styles and colors. If you want attractive containers, you still need conventional planters—unless you get one big enough to hide a plain, self-watering container inside. That's up to you and your wallet, of course.

Back to the Topsy Turvy Planter: I used a determinate tomato for this experiment, twin to one in a self-watering container. As with the hay bales, I got dramatically different results. The container plant was small and weak but fruitful, while the Topsy Turvy plant grew vigorous foliage but few fruits. This may be because it got dried out more than once. I had trouble calculating how often to water it between rainstorms, because you can't see the dirt or fit your hand into the top hole to finger-test for moisture. Also, we hung it high, out of line-of-sight in the normal traffic pattern of the garden, so more than once I forgot it was there.

It worked, though—enough to inspire me to try again next year, applying lessons learned. I still love the idea and want to make it work.

Rock Gardening

Perhaps "rock gardens" should be called "pocket gardens" for the pockets of soil that get wedged naturally, or by your hand, among the crevices and contours of a rocky ledge. They lend themselves to pockets of color, usually for shallow-rooted and creeping plants.

A vision in these parts is the creeping phlox that spreads pink, white, and lavender across dark outcrops in the springtime. Because our state is a rocky, slopey one, many gardeners tuck imaginative combos of flowers amid the rocks to bloom in season on otherwise untillable land. The countryside is crisscrossed with tumbled-down stone walls that once divided pastures but now sprout wildflowers or are coated with creepers; or, like the retaining wall below our driveway, shelter seeds that grow into columbine and bleeding heart, which emerge and bloom each summer then withdraw and shuffle themselves around to pop out of a different opening the next year.

Some ambitious folks create their own rock gardens by hauling and positioning boulders just so, then planting between them. More often, rock gardens are happy by-products of human inspiration or Nature's chance.

I've always been interested in rocks. Not as a geologist, but I love them, so whenever I travel I pick up rocks and bring them home. I've got rocks from Turkey, Europe and the British Isles, Senegal and Mauritania and the Canary Islands, and all but four states in the United States. My parents always had people from all over the world stay with us, which cultivated in me a love for cultures. That's why I taught social studies.

When my windowsills and counters ran out of space for the rocks, I added them to the retaining wall around the front and side of our house. The first layer of the wall is composed of massive boulders, the second of medium-size stones, and the top is my collection. When we are all gone, and nine hundred years from now when archeologists discover the pile, they will surely wonder what it is!

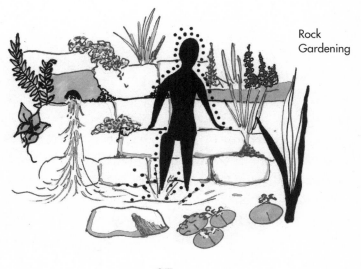

Rock
Gardening

I wanted a garden that wouldn't be like other people's gardens. This one started as a garden of rocks, then turned into a rock garden when I felt like growing some chives. I just moved a few rocks and added dirt between them. Later, at school, I won some yellow-bearded iris and the principal said, 'Just put them in your garden and forget about them.' I added them first to a vegetable garden, but they spread, and so I moved some to the wall. Now there are about twenty, including purple ones. Another time, an heirloom gardener who was training kids in transplanting brought some extras to the house, so we added them to the rock garden, too. And a former student brought me a chocolate mint to try putting into my cocoa. I put that in the rock garden, and it's now taken over the far corner!

Certain plants won't grow in the rock garden, I've discovered. But in general, anything that needs to be protected gets put in there, including more rocks, creating a one-of-a-kind garden of memories.

Patrice Ladd / Newport, Vermont

Community Gardening

Because not everyone has their own corner of land to work, especially in suburbs and cities, community gardens came into being. They live up to their name on two fronts. First, they are gardens open to members of a community, usually requiring some formality in order to secure your own plot. Second, they create their own community, one of gardeners sharing tools and labor and knowledge, as well as the gratification that comes from common interests and work toward the same goals.

Gardening is often a solitary pursuit, which is fine if retreat is what you're after. But even the most determined solo acts usually like to talk about their gardens with someone, sometime, if only to solve a technical problem. It helps a lot to swap tales, just like some people swap recipes. Some of my best garden days are when my mother and husband are out there with me, working on projects together. In community gardens, there's almost always another gardener around, with whom you can work in companionable quiet or share stories and discuss techniques. That person might be somebody you'd never talk with otherwise, and who, through your mutual interests, can become a helpful neighbor or a friend.

Most often, community garden plots are the traditional sort, though all the approaches discussed above can be implemented within their confines. It might be interesting to coordinate the members to each grow the same plants via different systems and compare results after harvest. I would enjoy such an opportunity, since working alone I must experiment one or two at a time over successive seasons, whose conditions vary from the year before. How nice to see if A worked better than B, C, or D, all in one season!

Comparisons happen naturally, albeit unsystematically, in a community garden, because the members bring their personal variables to the collective. This includes the downside, which is plots that run amok because the member(s) can't or won't keep up with the work after the initial zeal of planting. Fellow members can become disgruntled because the garden's aesthetics are ruined, or because sloppy housekeeping leads to insect infestations or disease. Therefore, community gardeners need to be team players or have a laissez-faire outlook in order to thrive in that scenario. It works like a family, or village, where people come to love and support each other despite any squabbles, knowing that their whole is greater than the sum of their parts.

Herb Gardening

For a long time I equated the word "garden" with flowers and vegetables. Then I expanded it to include fruits, since plenty of us grow berries or have a fruit tree, without getting into full orchards or vineyards. As a non-cook, non-craftsperson, I always forget about herbs, and when I do remember them, I mentally file them under flowers-and-foods.

But herbs have been making the world go round since the beginning of human history. Think about tea. Spices. Tobacco. Opium. Quinine. Hemp.

Herbs built the foundation of human culture and commerce, providing dyes and fibers, medicines and currencies. Technically, an herb constitutes any plant that isn't a shrub or tree, and in common parlance today refers to any plants grown for flavor and aroma rather than blossoms or nutrition. Culinary folks differentiate between herbs, grown for their leaves, and spices, grown for their nuts, roots, and berries. General gardeners often tuck herbs into a corner of their flower or vegetable plots, while people who don't garden at all might keep a pot of basil on the windowsill.

With herbs, you can grow an entire apothecary in your back-yard, or the base materials for weaving and dyeing. Or have a little market garden for specialty flavorings and scents. If nothing else, intermix herbs with your flowers and vegetables to attract good insects and repel bad ones. This works for you as well as your plants: common herbs such as garlic, cloves, lavender, lemon-grass, rosemary, thyme, and tansy are known to repel mosquitoes.

🍂 ✾ 🍂

I lived with my grandparents in Connecticut after graduation from college and they taught me how to garden. While there, I set up an art studio for my weaving and started dyeing yarns with dye plants I found in the woods and meadows.

Then I moved to the Southwest with my husband, and learned to dye using the plants that grew in a high-elevation mountainous environment. After we bought our own property, I began growing dye plants in my garden.

Now I market my own natural-dyed tapestry yarns. Since yarn stores have a limited color range, dyeing my yarn with natural dyes completes my color palette for my tapestries. I dry the dye-plant material on screens and by hanging because I'm too busy with the rest of the garden during the summer. Most of my dyeing takes place in the fall after the vegetable harvest is over. I love seeing the wonderful colors produced that match the hues of my surrounding environment. I usually have a chance to throw some of my own yarn into the dye pot other times during the year when I teach natural-dye workshops.

My favorite part, other than creating my tapestries, is the dyeing. It is an ancient science, and there was a time when certain dyes were more valuable than gold. Today I use plants like madder, goldenrod, asparagus fern, fennel, dark red hollyhocks, dahlias, coreopsis, cosmos, and leaves from apples, peaches, and plums to get my colors. If you're a dyer, you need to know what genus/species have the right chromophores to produce color on fiber.

Jane Hoffman / Alpine, Arizona

Landscape Gardening

It's hard to tell where the line falls between gardening and landscaping. In my mind, it's a matter of complexity and scale. The average gardener maintains a yard comprising a lawn and a garden, and deals with them separately. Food gardeners, in particular, tend to concentrate more on yield than cosmetic appeal. Landscape gardeners embrace the whole—grounds, house, outbuildings, masonry, statuary, water, season, audience, surrounding environment—and consider ambience, perspective, and relationship in their plans. They use the same concepts and much of the same vocabulary as interior designers.

I've heard some people describe their garden as a collection of outdoor rooms, which is just today's lingo for an old idea. Large gardens have always led somewhere and provided corners for contemplation, while changing color and fragrance and style over their course. Oriental gardens, in particular, meld art and spirituality into one sublime plan.

Some gardens start out as, well, just *gardens,* then grow into lifelong landscape projects as the gardener's hobby expands. I'm heading that direction, myself, now that I've got many acres to deal with of diverse character. Where a trowel was once enough tool, now I undertake projects that require a tractor, and I divide my time between garden, lawn, walls and walkways, trees, bushes, flowers, and vegetables. So when I claim to be gardening, what I really mean is, "I'm going outside to work around the yard."

Out there, I'm Mistress of the Universe. I can be as dominant and aggressive as I want ("Tree, I'm tired of your pine needles choking up my lawn and garden—be gone!") or as sentimental and undisciplined as I need ("This is my chance to create a wildlife sanctuary; I'll let that stand of goldenrod grow rather than mow it down because the finches will need the food in September"). I can stand on the hilltop and survey my domain, soaking in the beauty and the freedom it gives, and be a pioneer woman exulting in her triumph over the elements. Or I can just be a fool, and undertake relocating a pile of rocks to start a rustic border, and strain my back!

It turns out that I'm doing a lot of things, mostly subconscious, and not much to do with plants. I say this because I am repelled by gardening books, with their chapter-one mandate: 'First test the soil.' (No way! My approach to plants is to find the ones that will love the soil they are put in—so obviously I move things around and re-plant a *lot*.) For me, step one is staring and feeling the contours of a patch of ground—as in, which places want to be more and which places want to be less. I want to bring out the forms that are latent within the ground by using rock walls and paving stones and bric-a-brac and plants to enhance the lines and shapes. In other words, I am visualizing and channeling and sculpting and sewing (as in stitching) at the same time.

It's my grandmother's goldfish pond all over again, so perfectly nestled into a crook in the lower level of her yard, with daylilies arching over it. And her upside-down metal trash-can lids under the shrubbery, filled with water for bird baths. I imprinted on her yard, and at some young age had an epiphany that its spaces had been heightened by her hand.

All my senses are surging in harmony when I garden, and as I lay in bed this morning trying to put this sensation into words, I had the funny notion that it was a Celtic woman within me who was having this experience in the yard. And then I realized that this sensation is not different from what turned me on as a surficial geologist. In that job, I looked at landforms all day in order to discern their creation. And further still, I realized that maybe I love to do both geology and gardening because I have a Celtic sense of place, if you know what that means. And so the happy thought came to me that maybe I love to garden because it lets me keep practicing the art of landform analysis.

I am not an artist like so many in my family, but for me gardening is a creative process that comes from deep within and seeks expression as inevitably as water runs downhill. Judging from other people's reaction to my yard, quite a lot of what I see there is all in my head! Mine is not a classically gorgeous garden. But the people who like it can't explain why except to say that they feel something about it. Ahhhh . . .

So, having sworn we would never buy a house with a big yard again, what did we do two years ago? We bought a house with a big neglected yard overrun with weeds and littered with piles of limestone blocks from another demolished house. (Oh, and let's not forget the menacing tornado shelter and the looming stand of bamboo in the back!) It has been so much fun carving new gardens into the rough using the limestone. And I am so fortunate to have a husband who sees patios and pathways in his mind's eye wherever he looks; he has created some gorgeous shapes and spaces that flow through the yard. He too has vivid memories of childhood yards. In his case, he actually installed them with his father. So I guess that together we'll be conjuring up our landscapes of old well into our old age.

Elizabeth London / Norman, Oklahoma

FOUR

Something for Everyone

Connection with gardens, even small ones, even potted plants,
can become windows to the inner life. The simple act of stopping
and looking at the beauty around us can be prayer.

—PATRICIA R. BARRETT, *THE SACRED GARDEN*

Here's a thought that blows my mind every time I consider it: Everyone has different fingerprints. This is merely an interesting fact until you do the math. Ten fingers times how many millions of people? Yikes!

Likewise, every snowflake that falls from the sky is unique. That must add up to billions, maybe even trillions, every year around the world!

Armed with these two thoughts, you can't miss Nature's capacity for individualism. What it means for us here is: Anyone can be a gardener, on any scale, according to any taste, working with or around any limitations. Until I grasped this concept, I missed out on gardening's benefits because I believed that I needed a lot of space in which to dig, and that I had to commit myself to a gardening lifestyle. In truth, gardens fit into any lifestyle. You can pick the option that suits you like you might

pluck a grape from a vine. Then it's up to you whether you cultivate the vine to enjoy it visually; harvest the grapes to enjoy their
sweetness; or gear up and turn them into fine wine. I favor a mix
of vine and grapes, never mind the wine.

INDOOR GARDENING

So who needs a yard? A few pots and some commercial potting
soil bring all the garden one needs indoors. A larger investment
provides a greenhouse or atrium. As with outdoor gardens, your
own resources and character define the space and its denizens.

Houseplants offer visual, tactile, olfactory, and gustatory
pleasures. A vivid Gerbera daisy guarantees a smile. A geranium
gives color for weeks on end. A peace lily makes an elegant centerpiece, while an anthurium brings the tropics into any room.
Potted palms bracketing your favorite chair form a private
enclave, while African violets provide a range of exotic, lovely
flowers that will prosper in poor light. Aloe veras are virtually
indestructible and offer household first aid for burns and skin
conditions. A pot of oregano will flavor many a meal.

Familiar scents like jasmine, primrose, gardenia, begonia,
lavender come from plants of the same names known for their
aromas. All are good houseplants that can be grown year-round.
Fragrant rosemary trees do double duty: in addition to smelling
nice, they make good markers around the house if your vision is
impaired, and they can be trimmed into a conical shape as a substitute Christmas tree.

The classic holiday aroma, balsam, can be had all year in
sachets and draft stoppers after the real thing—Christmas trees,
wreaths, and garlands—have gone by. In spring, hyacinths and
Easter lilies fill a home with fragrance. Likewise with paper-
whites, which are miniature narcissi that can be "forced"

indoors. Normally done in the spring, bulb forcing can also be done all year if you buy a batch in season and store them in the refrigerator.

Cacti are the easiest keepers and many types reward you with flowers. A variety of foliage plants, such as rubber plants, snake plants, spider plants, ponytail palms, and rabbit foot ferns, help keep the air fresh in your dwelling and bring the outdoors inside. Everything in the bromeliad family makes

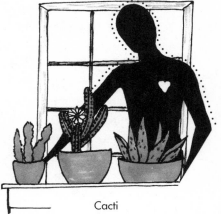

Cacti

good houseplants, ranging from the pineapple to Spanish moss and including "air plants" that thrive without soil. Orchids, too, can be grown this way, and—contrary to common belief—are simple to grow in apartment or household conditions.

If you want gorgeous blossoms *and* profuse foliage *and* perfume *and* edible fruit, train a passionflower to grow around your indoor space. Or you can go the opposite extreme, and cultivate the miniature trees known as bonsai.

I don't remember how old I was the first time I saw a picture of an orchid, maybe eight or ten. I think it was in a *National Geographic* magazine, probably in an article about Hawaii or South America. I just remember thinking *Someday I want to have one of those.* I was completely taken with their extraordinary and exotic appearance.

Many years passed, but I finally took the plunge and bought my first, a dendrobium in white with purple markings on the petals. I think I got it from the grocery store or a home improvement store, certainly not from a fancy florist or orchid grower. It has been repotted several times over the years and now fills a pot about ten inches across and blooms faithfully every year.

Of course, one can never have just one orchid; they seem to need company of their own kind, and so my collection has grown to six or seven, each one unique, each one my baby. Some have come to me as gifts, one from my mother, and one from a dear friend who has since passed away. Some have been spur-of-the-moment purchases, as my patient and understanding husband can attest. ("Do you really need another one?") One is even a souvenir from a trip to Florida we took one year in our motor home. It traveled all the way back to Connecticut in the bathtub!

I find orchids to be very resilient and forgiving plants. Sometimes I forget to water them for a week or more; they always seem to be fine. And I know they are supposed to be fertilized regularly, but somehow that never gets done. I place the pots on the front balcony of my condo for the summer where they are given an easterly exposure and filtered light by the use of roll-up blinds when the direct sun comes in the morning. They live there until just before the first frost then spend the winter in my living room in a west-facing window.

Each variety has its own bloom cycle. The first to arrive are the yellow Dancing Ladies, a whole chorus line of them on stems as long as four to six feet! The flowers really do look like tiny cancan dancers with frilly skirts and tiny waists.

They are followed by the phalaenopsis varieties, with large, flat, open flowers that some say look like giant moths. I have several in different colors—purple, white with yellow and fuchsia, lavender with purple markings—and then finally, the miniature phalaenopsis will bloom, lasting for most of the summer. It is truly amazing how long each blossom will last, many as long as two months. I have learned that proper pruning will encourage a rebloom within a few months to extend the bloom time even further. I never tire of admiring each individual blossom. They are each a work of art to me, so intricate and yet sturdy, almost waxy to the touch.

Recently I attended an orchid show and saw some of the most unusual orchids, most of which I never knew existed. Colors and shapes beyond anything I could have imagined. It was truly a temptation to take one (or more!) home. Maybe someday, when I have more space . . .

For now, my collection will have to remain somewhat limited, as there are plans to downsize even further to living in our motor home fulltime. And yes, I do intend to take them on the road with me. After all, I now know they travel in the bathtub just fine!

Diana Haley / Farmington, Connecticut

As with outdoor gardens, soil makes a large difference in indoor plant health and caretaking ease. Use a moisture-holding mix designed for indoor potting, and be attentive to size to prevent your plants from getting root-bound. Plants interact with their environments just like we do, so shuffle them around as necessary until hitting the right combination of light, water, container, food.

An often-overlooked option for indoor gardening is the terrarium, a miniature world in a greenhouse where you can create a complete landscape and follow its cycles. Doesn't matter what container you use—old aquarium or fishbowl, large jar or brandy snifter—as long as the glass is clear. You don't need to water

Indoor Gardening

often because a terrarium builds its own climate—allowing plants to grow that otherwise might not fare well in the dry environs of a home, especially in winter with the heat on, or during summer in the desert. You don't need full sunlight, either, since that will overcook the plants.

My personal dream is fresh tomatoes in December. I know it can be done but haven't quite worked out the logistics. Here in Zone Three, it will require a greenhouse or home remodeling. In the meantime, I just received an insert with a new magazine subscription, offering this gardening tip: "Snip a branch off a tomato plant in your garden, and put the stem in water until roots develop. Plant it in a pot you can bring into the house before the first frost . . . and you'll have fresh homegrown tomatoes even in the winter."

Hmm, looks like another experiment coming up!

WATER GARDENING

Ponds and Fountains

I suppose it's possible to have a water garden indoors—and surely someone does!—but for the most part this is a backyard enterprise, enhancing a regular garden or becoming its focal point. Either way, a garden pool offers an aesthetically pleasing place for contemplation as well as a home for aquatic life and a drinking spot for creatures of land and sky.

Since a half-acre pond came with our place, I let it be and concentrate on land gardening while it chugs along in an endlessly changing, condensed world involving rushes and wild iris, marsh marigolds, floating strands of I-don't-know-what, and surface algae, among which dragonflies skitter and frogs burp, minnows and tadpoles and fish dart in and out of shadows dodging the kingfishers and herons out to get them. At night, raccoons and weasels prey upon the freshwater shellfish, while migrating ducks touch down with a splash at dusk and dawn. I believe a pair of wood ducks has taken up nesting there, but they are so secretive I only glimpse them once or twice a summer.

A neighbor with a huge spread uses ponds as an excuse to exercise heavy equipment. He builds ponds for the sheer pleasure of it—up to four at last count. Conversely, a retired couple we know with a tiny backyard have installed, in the center of it, a preformed tiny pond with a tiny fountain. In the evenings they pull up lawn chairs and sit around it as if were a mountain lake and they were on vacation, sitting on the veranda of a cabin to enjoy the sunset view.

Which goes to show that you don't need acreage in order to experience the sounds of water and to savor the unique plants that go with it. Moving water, be it a chuckling stream, a soft rain, or the surf caressing the shore, invites us to pause and relax for a moment, to think warm thoughts or dream magical dreams. A private waterside retreat lets you recenter and rebalance yourself whenever you need it. That comfort is why some people buy "white noise" machines for home or office, where they can't hear real water. The trickle, or patter, or rhythmic muffled swish in the background eases away tension and, when installed in a bedroom, soothes them to sleep.

At the smallest scale of water gardening, you can install a self-contained tabletop or floor-standing fountain. Then there are container water-gardens appropriate for patios, and closed-loop systems that allow waterfalls and streams without a pond to catch them. When space and inclination allow, you can size up with kits or by old-fashioned digging, and build streams and waterfalls into the design.

Installing a water garden is a gratifying project for the technically minded. It involves basic engineering and lots of gizmos: pumps, liners, filters, landscaping materials, specialized pots and soils, and of course appropriate plants. Variations include the bog garden and pebble garden. The latter, with fountain, is about the easiest way to get into waterscapes. Pebble gardens require little space and simple installation, and provide a rustic, artistic look popular with children (and dogs, who love to drink from the spray!). Alternatively, bog gardens can be created to stand alone or adjoin a pond, but they need lots of rich soil, whereas a pond needs much less organic matter. A bog garden is essentially waterlogged soil supporting plants such as arrowhead, dwarf cattail and bamboo, bog orchids, aquatic mint, and other unusual specimens. They attract fluttering beauties like butterflies, dragonflies, and hummingbirds, along with frogs and turtles.

In a true pond, you can add fish. Koi are the most popular, owing to their size, vivid colors, and friendliness. Goldfish do well in a wide range of water conditions, and are so hardy, so easily obtained, and come in so many sizes and shapes that they are the starter fish of choice for new pond owners. More-exotic options exist for the dedicated hobbyist, and some folks stock their ponds with game fish. Fish, of whatever type, add to a water garden's enchantment. Remember to build in something for shelter, so your fish don't end up feeding the local birds, cats, and raccoons!

Enthusiasts refer to their hobby tongue-in-cheek as "pondering." The lifestyle emphasizes a spiritual haven centered around a pool or stream, embraced by a garden. While most everyone relaxes when sitting at waterside, ponderers make that a priority in their lives, because of the peace it brings them. They banish troubles and demands to outside the garden perimeter until recharged enough to address them.

I watch my own pond from the house, since we keep the

perimeter ungroomed in order to attract wildlife. It works: Each year, at least once, I dash inside to grab binoculars when an osprey dives in with a splash, or visiting migrants glide out of the rushes at twilight, quacking softly. And each spring, in an annual ritual, we paddle across to see if the fish survived, rejoicing when they suddenly appear in a semicircle around the boat to stare up at us. The spring peepers start up their chorus shortly after. By midsummer, you can hear frogs plopping into the water any time you approach.

Hydroponics

The more utilitarian version of water gardening is hydroponics: growing plants in a nutrient-enriched liquid. This spares you the vagaries of soil and weather and pests, though you still have to work with chemistry and plumbing. These days many commercial food products and nursery plants are grown hydroponically. Arizona hosts the largest such facility in the world, Eurofresh Farms—which perhaps should be called Eurofresh Greenhouse, for it has more than 250 glass-enclosed acres growing over 125 million pounds of tomatoes!

Thankfully, the home gardener can work on a simpler scale, using mason jars or plastic dishpans filled with inert, easy-to-obtain materials (rock wool, clay pebbles, gravel, perlite, vermiculite, sand, or foam chips) to support the plants, then periodically flooding and draining them with liquid nutrients. Starter kits using gravity feed are available for well under a hundred dollars. As with water gardens, you can step up in complexity to a fully automated setup. Maybe this is my route to year-round tomatoes . . .

Aeroponics work the same way as hydroponics, except that the plant roots are nourished by a mist instead of a liquid. (In case you're wondering, "geoponics" is the term for regular gardening in soil.) Air and water gardening are great for folks who like things tidy or wish to avoid the physicality of conventional gardening. These options incur startup and maintenance costs, as all gardening does, but still allow an interaction with plants that can enrich your life.

THEME GARDENING

Railroad Gardens

As with the hay bales and Topsy Turvy planter, I stumbled upon railroad gardens while looking for something else. Now I'm convinced that gardens truly offer something for everyone!

An extension of the model train hobby, railroad gardening has grown to become a family recreation. The term "garden railroad" originated in England in the 1860s, where "garden" was the British term for what Americans call a backyard. Railroad gardening has since come to include gardens as a key component in constructing a miniature landscape. Hence the family appeal. One member builds and manages the trains and tracks; another designs, plants, and maintains the greenery (often using dwarf trees and shrubs, or else artful pruning); another builds the terrain, waterscapes, and structures. Then, if the scale of the model railroad can accommodate it, everyone takes a ride.

For the most part, garden railroads are too small for riding, being outdoor model-train setups. The larger ones are dubbed "backyard railroads" and have their own culture and criteria. Garden railroads tend to be magnificent projects—often a life's work—necessitating show-and-tell. Thus, garden railroad clubs and societies invite each other to social gatherings, and rotate the sites of their meetings. The grander displays get installed at expos and botanical gardens to wow the public.

Topiary

If you're artistically inclined and not into machinery, try topiary. This is sculpture with plants, using clipped, evergreen shrubs and trees, most commonly arborvitae, box, holly, yew, and privet. People have been doing it since Roman times, creating animals, geometric forms, and labyrinths. You can do it with houseplants, too—the principles are the same.

First train a plant around a frame into the form you want, then prune and trim it as it fills out, limiting growth to about three inches from the frame. This constitutes two-dimensional or shrub topiary; the three-dimensional version, or sphagnum topiary, depends entirely on the shaped frame and needs to be stuffed with sphagnum moss. Topiary calls for simple tools, such as snippers, wire frames, fishing line, hairpins, and watering paraphernalia. Maintenance is minor but continual, so it's a great thing to do if you like to dabble.

Topiary

Historically, topiary gardens have highlighted the grounds of grand estates, mainly in Europe. Some of these gardens have been maintained for hundreds of years. One of the oldest in America is the Green Animals Topiary Garden in Portsmouth, Rhode Island. Its topiary comprises nearly a hundred trees on seven acres, forming a menagerie of bears, a camel, a giraffe, an ostrich, an elephant, a pineapple, a unicorn, a reindeer, a dog, plus a horse and rider. A younger but perhaps grander topiary can be found at the Walt Disney World Resorts in Florida and California. These incorporate many famous cartoon characters into their designs. In topiary, you are limited only by your imagination.

BACKYARD ORCHARDS

Fruits and berries epitomize summer, seeming to capture all the wonder of sunshine and warmth. That makes them the highlight of the season in the North Country, and a signature product and industry in the south. Anywhere in the country, serious backyard food gardeners usually include a fruit tree or berry patch in their holdings. In some cultures, a backyard orchard is a way of life.

California exemplifies the backyard orchard lifestyle. Although much of the state's early population went there for gold, it was also settled by folks who raised living gold—grapes and oranges. Their descendants instilled a "fruit-tree mentality" throughout the state that makes it a leading producer today. Its long, narrow shape along the Pacific coast, with inland mountains, includes the warmest growing zones, enhanced by microclimates. So Californians can grow everything from tropical fruits to the stone fruits that require a cool season to set.

Settlers from the East were thrilled to have citrus available. Many of them became co-op growers for Sunkist, which would pick the growers' acreage and give them a percentage of crop value. This practice held from the 1920s until the 1950s, when shifting economics made picking small plots unviable. But family orchards remained; traditionally, trees near the house for daily diet—orange, peach, plum, apricot—and a secondary group for specialties—clementine, avocado, kiwi, sapote—that either ripen too quickly to survive in a marketplace, or are too exotic to find in the market, or are cheaper to grow than to buy.

Immigrants with fruit-growing history clustered in hospitable California, and even today stamp their enclaves with their favored fruits: calamansi for Filipinos; wampi, longan, and lychee for Asians; papaya, mango, and banana for Central and South Americans; figs, pomegranates, and quince for Armenians; olives and grapes for Mediterraneans.

For the broad American population, backyard orchards faded with improved technology, meaning better commercial production and distribution of fresh fruit, which brought availability up and prices down. Fruit trees that had fed the family were replaced by swimming pools and ornamental gardens during the consumer-growth period of the 1950s through the 1970s.

The advent of dwarf varieties, however, especially citrus, returned fruit to the backyard. Compact size and attractive evergreen foliage made fruit trees a lovely, fragrant ornamental. And as fruit prices rose again, more and more options for grow-it-yourself came available, followed by interest in sustainable agriculture and organic farming methods. Nowadays people again grow their own food, and share or sell the surplus.

I'm passionate about quince.

"What? You're passionate about what?" most folks ask.

Quince.

"Spell it?"

Q-U-I-N-C-E.

"Fifteen? You're passionate about the number fifteen?" a Spanish-speaking friend puzzled, thinking me a *gringa* communicating in Spanglish.

"Not *quince* (keen-say). *Membrillo* (mem-bree-oh)," I said in my most articulate Spanish.

"Ah! *Membrillo*. I love *membrillo*."

Coing in French, *quitte* in German, *ayva* in Turkish—across the globe, the fruit-bearing quince tree (*Cydonia oblongata*) is cultivated and prized for its versatility in the kitchen. But here in the United States, the quince has been nearly forgotten.

It's hard to imagine a time when this aromatic relative of the apple and pear was a centerpiece on the American table. But the astringent fruit with limited snacking appeal was so valued for its high pectin content and cooked musky flavor that settlers brought it to New England in 1629. Soon, however, the apple snatched the spotlight and the popularity of quince steadily declined. The development of artificial pectin in the mid-twentieth century sounded the death knell for the quince in the United States. Today the fruit is listed as a rare, specialty fruit.

My passion for the fruit was kindled as a child. Everyone in my family was weaned on Grandma's delicious ruby-red quince preserves. We had quince trees growing in the yard, and every fall my grandmother watched the fruit for sign of ripening. She taught me that the rock-hard fruit was ready for picking when its fuzzy green skin turned yellow and the heady, rose-like fragrance of quince permeated the neighborhood. For days before she made her preserves and jelly, baskets brimming with ripening quince would sit in the hallway and the aroma of quince filled the house. In ancient times, Greeks placed ripe quinces in their closets as fresheners. After my grandmother passed away, I gladly took on the family tradition of *quincing*—with one major difference: I invited other cooks to participate.

Autumn quincing events became a tradition in my own home, and each year I've expanded my repertoire of quince dishes to include savory stews, sauces, and glazes for roasted meats, unique dressings, and a wide variety of desserts—lots and lots of desserts—all perfect for holiday feasts and giftgiving.

Whether fueled by fond memories or unique culinary delights, my need to champion the underdog fruit developed into a passion.

I decided to plant a quince tree in Rhode Island, not far from Anne Hutchinson's colony of quince-loving settlers. A delicately branched bare-root seedling arrived from Pennsylvania, and a gardening buddy helped me dig a hole in a sunny, sea-breeze-protected location generous enough to accommodate a full-sized tree.

Within days of planting, a network of neighbors, friends, and fruit growers from Rhode Island to Vermont to Philadelphia began taking an interest in the little tree's health and survival. Neighbors offered to water it in my absence, and they began to take pictures and send me progress reports. "The quince tree has leaves!" said one neighbor. An overly optimistic update even claimed the young tree had a tiny blossom. Once established, quince trees do have pretty white or pink spring blossoms. Soon names poured in—Quincy, Dr. Quince, and my favorite, QT. Just as quince preserve-making had become a group culinary tradition in my kitchen, now a community had united around looking after the little quince tree in Rhode Island.

Reestablishing the quince's rightful place in the garden and on the table seemed daunting at first. But, today, when someone asks "What's a quince?" I invite them to join the growing number of gardeners and foodies committed to cultivating and cooking the quintessential fruit.

Barbara Ghazarian, The Queen of Quince /
Pacific Grove, California

Fruit trees require steady maintenance, especially pruning, for which the gardener is rewarded with tree-ripe, delicious fruit. For a prolonged harvest in the confines of a yard, plant the trees close together—ideally, several varieties that ripen at different times, which have the same service requirements—and keep them small (no taller than you standing with your arms extended). A two-for-one trick is to establish a fruit hedge to cover fencing or create a privacy screen. You can grow trees in containers as well; for instance, a personal supply of sweet Meyer lemons or Valencia oranges, even your own miniature coffee plantation. Just be sure to mount the containers on rolling stands, unless you have a forklift available to move them!

Thanks to mobile containers, northern gardeners can grow citrus fruit, as long they move the trees inside during winter. In the south, it works in reverse: many of the stone fruits that flourish in the north, such as apples, peaches, pears, plums, and apricots, don't do well because they need a chilly period as part of their production cycle. So southerners must grow special varieties adapted for their climates, or do without.

Grapes go both ways, so they can be grown around the country as long as you work with the appropriate variety. Choose from among the two major grape groups: Concord (the main type available in the East) and European vinifera (the main type available in the West). The drooping Concord types are what you usually see in grape arbors, whereas the climbing European vinifera type is what you usually see in vineyards. Note that table grapes make poor wine, and wine grapes make for poor eating, so you need to cultivate the proper type to get the desired result.

The Concord grape, by the way, is one of only three native North American fruits that are grown commercially. The other two are the blueberry and the cranberry. Blueberries are popular for backyard growing, along with raspberries, and will produce generously without pruning or spectacularly with all the right care. Cranberries, a bog plant, are hard to come by for the home grower. Nevertheless, these too can be cultivated in a personal garden, as more and more people are doing now that they've discovered the high nutrition value of cranberries—and blueberries, as well. This native American trio would make a good theme garden. All you cooks out there who enjoy home canning and preserve-making might consider that idea.

Back to grapes: The vines are like fruit trees, in that they need regular maintenance. Lazy gardeners like me lack the patience for all this, though I can understand how the close interaction between plant and gardener over many years can engage one's mind and heart (especially when the reward comes as fine wine!). I perceive grapes with an unromantic eye, contemplating them as potential pest control. I've heard that they are favored by Japanese beetles, so the thought of luring my nemesis away from the vegetable and flower gardens to a grape arbor holds appeal. (My Armenian friend, who collects young grape leaves in the spring for cooking, would gasp at the thought.)

Unfortunately, I don't have anything in the yard for the grapes to climb, and need my spouse's help to construct an arbor. Perhaps when he finishes all the home- and shop-related construction projects that are taking priority . . .

. . . although when that fine day comes, I'll probably ask for a greenhouse, first!

❀　　❀　　❀

As you see from all of the above, the living green world offers many ways to enjoy its beauty and produce. Those of us already bitten by the gardening bug usually mix and match from the list. I find that the combination of creating a private Eden and nursing living beings, along with physically expressing my ideas, provides an occupation that soothes yet stimulates—and keeps surprising me with the doors it opens. Although more than once I've been driven to tears by my gardening efforts, those experiences have taught me something no other aspect of life has succeeded in teaching: patience. Then, in spite of my mistakes, plants recover and regrow, showing silent forgiveness. This moves me to forgive myself, which builds greater patience with and willingness to forgive others. Ultimately, the garden teaches humility, for you can't control a microcosm of nature any more than you can control the primeval force behind it. So to find joy in a garden you must work with it, not against it. It will become your place of peace when you reach a dynamic balance. You can be your honest self there and work in direct give-and-take with the greatest power.

I grew up hating gardens. Dad had a big one nearly every year, and we all had to work in it. There's nothing worse than harvesting prickly-itchy okra on a hot, humid Alabama day just after a rain. The weeds are mile high, and the mosquitoes are buzzing in your hair. After years of it, I swore up and down I'd never have a garden when I was grown, and I meant it.

I grew up and kept my word. I moved to the city and lived where I couldn't have a hope of a garden. All my produce came from a garden planted by someone else, weeded by someone else, and harvested by someone else. I just had to bag it and take it to the checkout line. No mosquitoes, no prickles, no humidity.

Then a pregnancy ended with a loss. The physicians told me to take it easy until my body could heal. I lay on the couch day in and day out, taking meds, pushing away meals, accepting injected meds, waiting until the day the doctor would pronounce me well enough to move on. Television was boring. There was nothing I wanted to read. There was only the window beside the couch. I watched the rain. I watched the street go through its day. Mostly I watched this square of grass in front of my apartment.

Misery has to go somewhere, and I found myself wanting to plant that space. When I was able to get up, I went outside and surveyed this tiny spot. I borrowed a shovel and turned over the grass. Neighbors came over as I worked, and we talked about gardening as I sectioned the spot off into square-foot blocks. Because it was too early to plant anything else, I planted sugar snap peas and snow peas in each block, following guidelines I read in Mel Bartholomew's book. When the first tendrils emerged, I was thrilled. Each day, I checked on their progress. They grew taller and claimed this spot of land as theirs.

It snowed. Not just a light snow, but a snow that brought along an ice storm that induced power outages. My area, unused to this kind of weather, was stunned. My children and I huddled for days under blankets, doing all we could to keep warm. I figured my garden was dead. Days later, when the weather warmed some, the snow melted, and the power returned, I went outside to look at the remains of my garden.

It wasn't dead.

The snow peas were still vibrant and thriving in the patches of snow.

Since then, I have always had some form of a garden. Gardening sustains me. It reminds me that in the darkest of times there is always hope, and that I should always believe in the tenacity of life.

Barbara Merchant / Covington, Georgia

FIVE

The Fruits of Other People's Labor

If you'd have a mind at peace, a heart that cannot harden,
go find a door that opens wide upon a little garden.

—E. M. BOULT

ou don't have to actually garden to gain the benefits of gardening. In the same way that artists and performers need an audience in order for their work to be complete and their souls to be fulfilled, gardens need to be observed and appreciated by someone beyond the force that created them. So by merely paying attention to plants, we participate in a positive exchange.

Other people's gardens provide refreshment that's hard to resist because of the energy they exude. A garden captures and emanates the labor and love put into it by the gardener(s), as well as the vigor of the plants themselves and the dynamic created by their struggle to survive and reproduce. The by-product of their efforts—flowers, fruits, herbs, and vegetables—present us with beauty and wholesome food as well as a place to recharge.

Gardens are a gift we can receive almost anywhere we go,

whether or not they cost money to experience. But there's plenty out there for free, thanks to Ma Nature and gardening enthusiasts, the fruit of whose labors can be found wherever we look.

It may seem, sometimes, that the industrialized world has damaged so much of the natural world that it will never recover. I used to fear that, but the sight of a weed breaking through concrete allays my fears every time. And to stop myself from worrying about overpopulation, I look around at the gardens that so many people create. In every village, town, and city, in every country, people keep the earth alive through their plantings. By such signaling of hope and fellowship through living beauty, I feel compelled to do same in return.

For over a century Elizabeth Park has been an oasis where the city of Hartford opens to the skies. With over a hundred acres, there is space to gather together or find a solitary spot for enjoyment.

I go there often, and each time I give thanks for gardeners. I'm an appreciator, not a gardener. I've managed to kill cacti with my black thumb. Having failed miserably at gardening, I understand the time and effort required to keep these extensive public lands in beautiful condition.

A flock of professionals tends to springtime bulbs, thousands of summer roses, season-spanning annuals, perennials, rock gardens, flowering shrubs, and through the landscape a collection of rare and unusual trees. And here is a home for the displaced gardener who has lost his plot. The conservators of this space include a volunteer force of lay-gardeners, The Friends of Elizabeth Park. All work in harmony to bring our public park to us in its full beauty.

As I roam the gardens through their cycles finding joy in each blossom and birdcall, I say from my heart, "thank you, gardeners."

Caroline Hewitt / Hartford, Connecticut

PRIVATE AND POTLUCK GARDENS

Depending on where you live, a stroll can present myriad garden experiences. The same is true on your daily walk to the mass transit station or dash from the parking lot to your office or the store. People stick gardens anywhere they will grow!

In Town

I'm particularly fond of fire-escape gardens in cities. Twelve stories up there will be tomatoes growing in buckets beneath laundry hanging out to dry. Some enterprising residents on the top floor might lay out whole rooftop gardens, which sometimes can be glimpsed from the street. In the same vein, big corporations are starting to jump onto the "green" bandwagon and converting the desert acreage of their flat roofs to burgeoning gardens.

Lucky you if you work for one of those outfits!

China, fast becoming the world leader in carbon dioxide emissions, is countering that trend by becoming a leader in restoring its cities and countryside. Back in 1981, the government decreed that all citizens ages eleven to fifty-five must plant three to five trees every year, resulting in billions of trees restored to the planet. Then, motivated by the 2008 Olympics in Beijing, government and

Fire-escape Garden

university officials organized the Green Long March, modeled after the historic Long March in the 1930s. In the Green March, thousands of students and environmental activists traveled the country teaching the people how to live and conduct business in a sustainable fashion.

Bolstered by movements like this around the globe as well as ongoing pressures since the 1970s to address green concerns here, U.S. municipalities have become more conscious of the need for street-side beauty and the air-cleansing ability of plants. "Little elves" now spend their time beautifying the cityscape when we're not looking so we'll have something to enjoy when we lift our eyes. Whether municipal employees or contract landscape services, environmental zealots or just garden club volunteers, these workers maintain pocket gardens all over town. These can be traffic islands, sidewalk planters, and hanging baskets trailing bright flowers and foliage, changed for each season. Many cities install hardy tree specimens to line their sidewalks, providing flowers and shade.

Hanging Baskets

To the best of my knowledge, every city, and almost every town, contains a park, be it just a square or a residual town green, or something magnificent like New York's Central Park. Even in the most cement-and-concrete jungle, plants are everywhere, if only in whiskey barrel planters outside shopkeepers' doors. Street vendors sell bouquets: in the city, from carts along the walkways; in the country, from the backs of trucks parked in sidings. And in cities, towns, and hamlets all over, savvy merchandisers ornament their window displays with plants.

Savvy builders go the same route to a greater degree with landscaping. Borders around shopping plazas and parking lots contain spectacular beds of color three seasons of the year, and foliage interest during the fourth. Highway crews now plant wildflower meadows in the medians of interstates, or cover steep banks with flowering shrubs. In Hartford, Connecticut, when the highway was put through the city, they used forsythia for erosion control. Now, every springtime, those steep banks become a yellow blaze lining the high-speed curves into the city. I'm surprised there aren't more traffic accidents as people stomp on the brakes and stare!

In southern Vermont, where a main artery slices between hills, there's a similar sight in late summer when a slope erupts into a blanket of black-eyed Susans. Then, of course, there's foliage season in the fall, when the New England hills are electrified with colors and the roads jam up with "leaf peepers." Autumn in general is one of the best times to view gardens, as plants put on a last fiesta of blossom, leaf, or vegetable, and the summer extremes of heat and bugs abate.

There are good and bad things about living in a resort town. The bad thing is that you have to drive twenty-three miles to the nearest Kmart if you want to buy anything without a designer label on it; the cost of gas being far less than the cost of the item if forced to buy it on your home turf.

But one of the good things about a resort town is that they are usually alive with fabulous gardens. Manchester, where I lived for a time in southern Vermont, is no exception. Starting in spring, Manchester is one big flower garden.

Nestled into a narrow verdant valley in the Green Mountains, the town's beauty has made it a real-estate hot spot for wealthy retirees and just as wealthy refugees fleeing the big city. They plant themselves here and then cultivate their property, hiring landscape gardeners to create picture-perfect landscapes. And that is just fine with me because these new house-proud residents display all of this floral bounty at the front of their property where the rest of us can enjoy it. A more reticent and private bunch, we resident Yankees—myself included—cultivate traditionally, which means we grow gardens out back where no one else can see them. This makes the exuberant displays by our new neighbors very much appreciated.

The town's businesses believe in gardens, too. These establishments—decorators, gift shops, restaurants, and our wonderful independent hardware store—are joined by a plethora of high-end national brand outlets here to lure skiers and summer visitors. They do it with the finery in their windows and the beauty of the landscape out front. Our town selectmen showed great wisdom when they forced these chains to build vernacular buildings that hug the street. With sidewalks at their doorsteps and car parks hidden behind, the greenways between sidewalk and street are used to advantage, cultivated with glorious, well-tended blooming annuals and perennials. Storefront windows add to this green display. Old-fashioned wooden window boxes are replanted every spring with flowering annuals and are replenished to bloom continually as the seasons progress. Large planters sit next to benches under tree-shaded paths to the side of these stores. This is where husbands perch, patiently waiting for their wives to max out their credit cards.

Added to all of this riotous floral beauty, the town parks and green spaces are planted with lilies, roses, and flowering shrubs. A walk here is a feast of color and scent, like taking a free garden tour any day of the week. So while I may not be able to buy a new frying pan down the block, I sure can smell the roses.

Leslie Noyes / Bennington, Vermont

All year long, I love to walk in cemeteries. They are beautiful and restful, and available in almost any community. By viewing them from the perspective of life instead of death, I see them as gardens of memory and symbols of continuity. The grave markers often show creative artistry in the monuments themselves as well as the plantings around them. (One cemetery I walk in has an oil painting on canvas propped up at a gravesite, instead of a stone marker, showing figures standing together overlooking a special view. It riveted me in place the day I first saw it, and I always pause and look when I go by. The caretaker tucks it away for the winter, during which it haunts me with pleasurable mystery.)

All cemeteries abound with floral displays during the growth season. Some cemeteries ban live plants, others ban artificial ones; neither policy stops people from leaving imaginative and deeply personal tokens of their love. Other cemeteries are gardens in themselves, rife with flowering bulbs and shrubs, bordered by evergreens and hardwoods. The grounds are usually groomed into park-like settings, through which meandering pathways make good places to walk. If you live in or visit southern New England, you'll find a stellar example of cemetery-park-arboretum at Mount Auburn Cemetery in Cambridge, Massachusetts.

Mount Auburn was the first major-scale designed landscape in the United States, opened to the public back in 1831. A model for parks and cemeteries nationwide, it is, perhaps, the Ultimate Garden—bringing together past, present, and future in its preservation of historic buildings and reverence of people who have gone before us, while celebrating life, art, and architecture through its monuments, collections, and plantings. The cemetery covers 175 acres of hills and dales, including ponds and fountains, lawns, gardens, and forests, supporting thousands of species from around the globe. People go there to bird-watch and study horticulture, as well to attend lectures and recitals, and cruise through in their cars or on foot, looking around in awe. Although still an active cemetery, it serves more as park and education center—and urban oasis. It is open every day, all year, and accessible for free.

Out of Town

My all-time favorite outing is what my spouse calls "a drive-about." These days it's hard to justify the fuel cost (and it's rapidly becoming socially frowned upon to expend such fuel for recreation), but a drive is still one of the most benignly enjoyable pastimes available. When I'm super-busy, I need the break. When bored and lonely, I get revived by a change of scenery. Always I find something intriguing, or at least different, in a jaunt out of town.

I've noticed that even in heavily settled areas, plants define the character of the landscape. Indeed, they declare identity as much as any color of paint. In suburban developments, where so many houses look alike, owners distinguish their plots with ornamentals. Out in the country, where zoning is less strict (and the press for residential conformity less intense), the homes themselves come in diverse—and sometimes strange—form, with yards just as distinct.

As I noodle around, I note that some places have grand, old trees framing the house, and out back a vegetable garden fortified by deer fencing. In front, mature flowering shrubs and crafted beds bloom in color-coordinated sequence through the seasons. Some people mow their lawn down to an emerald velvet while others let the yard run crazy. Some clear their view line, whereas others block it with a palisade of trees. And some folks consider "stuff" decoration and let the wildflowers grow right through it.

Wildflowers to some, weeds to others—"What we call a weed is in fact merely a plant growing where we do not want it," said E. J. Salisbury (*The Living Garden*, 1935). I'm of the wildflower camp and adore seeing them wherever they want to grow, despite all we do to discourage them. Happily, they are free to colonize roadside scruff and to spiral up phone poles and guy wires. In fact, certain plants grow only in disturbed ground, so good luck getting them into your garden.

Take chicory, for example. I tried to grow it in my garden, but it didn't like the rich loamy bed. I tried again in the gravelly edge of the driveway. Nope: wasn't wasteland enough. Give it highway shoulders, where it can run for miles in unbroken strips of periwinkle blue. Chicory also flourishes in forgotten grubby corners of parking lots, construction sites, and abandoned buildings. Likewise, staghorn sumac springs up in humankind's wake. I often see handsome plantations of sumac along roadsides and growing up through ruined buildings, as well as in the middle of our partially collapsed stone wall.

Over time, as my interest in plants has grown, concurrent with an interest in birds and geology, I've started seeing the landscape as a patchwork quilt of habitats. The land's contours correlate with colors, which correlate in turn with the plants that thrive in each niche. Soon I learned that areas around running water and standing water and salt water host specific groups, just as altitude and soil define what can grow. On long drives you can watch grass give way to scrub, then to scrubby woods, then pure forest, which becomes interspersed with evergreens until suddenly the landscape becomes evergreen-only, with the trees shrinking as you climb. Then, abruptly, that invisible zone called "the tree line" appears, beyond which only the hardiest ground-hugging plants can survive.

I first encountered the tree line on Mount Washington in New

Hampshire. It lies at about 5,000 feet. Years later, in Montana, I found myself at 7,000 feet but still surrounded by forest. Apparently the tree line is not an arbitrary altitude but a relative one for each area. (Big clue for gardening experiences yet to come!)

Trees also illustrate the prevailing winds. On harsh coastlines or inland plains, the few trees bend in the same direction, telling a story. A different story is told by lone-sentinel elm trees in the Northeast. That species got wiped out in the mid-1900s by the Dutch elm disease. Yet individual elms far apart still live, a wine-glass-shaped silhouette against the sky. Coming upon one always chokes me up a bit. So does an empty bird's nest exposed in a tree after the leaves have fallen. Conversely, my heart sings upon seeing a valley filled solid with blooming color, or late autumn fields lit up gold by sunbeams slanting in beneath slaty clouds.

Winter is long here in northern New England. Come spring, days lengthen and begin to warm as we wait impatiently for what Vermonters call "mud season" to dry out enough to allow us to wander outdoors without danger of becoming mired to our knees in what would be hard-packed roadbed in other seasons. So it was, almost twenty years ago, that the soil finally changed back from mud soup into solid ground and my three-year-old and I ventured forth, walking along the dirt road in front of our house. Inquisitive as only toddlers can be, she wanted to know the name of every flowering plant we saw. I didn't have the answers. My knowledge, left over from childhood flower picking, included hardly more than the names of daisies, black-eyed Susans, and Queen Anne's lace.

As we walked, I noticed a happy example of our environment being a little better off than it used to be. With the demise of DDT (a toxic insecticide) and a new awareness that wildflowers are beautiful and economical to grow, when compared to the cost of mowing hundreds of miles of roadside, a greater variety of wildflower species grow here than when I was small. Walking hand in hand with my questing daughter that spring, we bent to examine interesting red and blue flowering grasses as well as other plants that flourished in the meadows and along the roadside near our house. Thus I came to own Peterson's *Field Guide to Wildflowers,* my first nature guidebook.

It still pleases me to remember the plant names we learned together and to mark their sighting now, long after my toddler has become a beautiful young woman and the chubby little hand that held mine so tightly has grown long and elegant. I still take walks, but now it is my dog accompanying me. Naming the wildflowers has become an important way for me to mark the seasons: Ah, there is the bloodroot of early spring—that means the marsh-marigolds will be along soon. Around the same time, as the earth warms, coltsfoot appears then goes quickly to seed. The insects begin to chirp and sing around the time the vivid periwinkle chicory blooms, flourishing in the poor sandy soil along the edge of the road, and goat's-beard waves bright yellow in the meadows.

So it goes, flowers marking the passage of summer, rose mallow and the round dusty pink globes of milkweed flowers giving way to a profusion of yellow-green cowparsnip. Still later, the red raspberry bushes bloom with deep pink flowers and hot summer days erupt in stands of goldenrod. The goldenrod, blooming in the first week of August, seems to come too soon, for its appearance means that fall isn't far behind. Nights turn suddenly cooler. Though there is still plenty of summer left, crisper, clearer days slip in among the hot humid ones and purple asters, the last flowers of summer, bloom. Late summer is purple and gold here in Vermont as bushy aster plants preen amidst the goldenrod in browning fields. As beautiful as the asters are, they make me melancholy because true fall must soon follow—and as those of us living in these sublimely beautiful Green Mountains know, close around the bend in the road, our next long, gray winter awaits.

Leslie Noyes / Bennington, Vermont

Enjoying the fruits of other people's labor can be a literal as well as visual experience. Farmstands and country stores sell fresh produce superior to any supermarket offering: corn, tomatoes, cucumbers, peppers, squash; fruits and berries, pumpkins, maple syrup, jams, and pies. Many vineyards offer tours and free samples. I know people who organize a day's outing or a week's vacation around such food stops. They've learned yet another way to let the plant world enhance their lives.

Around the Corner

Some people engage with plants as entertainment. Searching out species and hybrids around the neighborhood becomes a treasure hunt, challenging to do on one's own or fun to do with a friend. Here in Vermont we have the Vermont Tree Society, which maintains a running list of the largest trees in the state and collects their stories. In all fifty states, enthusiasts hunt Big Trees—the champions in size and spread—and compete with each other in locating them. Their findings get channeled into the National Register of Big Trees, managed by a private forest conservation organization, American Forests.

Whether you concentrate on trees, garden plants, or wildflowers, learning to identify everything you see adds intellectual stimulation to your life. Plant ID takes either a good guidebook or the nerve to speak with strangers—asking proprietors, groundskeepers, or passersby if they know what that flower is. Sometimes the exchange creates new friendships. If nothing else, plant hunting provides fresh air and exercise, and better acquaints one with the neighborhood. Also, it creates opportunity to encounter something interesting along other lines.

Dog walkers know all about this. Long established as a way to meet people and get to know your turf, dog-walking forces you to pause and look around, and often to follow unplanned paths as the doggy nose pursues a trail you can't sense. These are golden moments to zero in on the plants around you, especially since the walking ritual is already part of your day.

I don't have a dog, so I achieve the same end through solo walking. By covering the same ground every day I've come to know my plant-ly neighbors, and enjoy watching their cycles of life. Just down the road there's the private club of trilliums. They convene at the base of a particular tree, a huge, craggy sugar maple, for a week or two each May. Then there are the refugee camps—bishop's weed and myrtle escaped from a garden long gone and now covering, respectively, a quadrant of shade beside a barn, and flowing out of the foundation of a ruined silo. Further on, at the edge of a sunny meadow, is the white flower encampment. I've never figured out what they are, but they sure like that chunk of ground near the drainage ditch. Birds and deer like the ancient apple tree that struggles on where pasture meets forest (and loses a bit more to it each year). That remnant of somebody's orchard still produces gnarly fruit despite being at least a hundred years old.

My human neighbors, meanwhile, express themselves through window boxes cascading petunias or dooryard gardens bristling with herbs, not to mention favorite blossoms artfully arranged around birdbaths, sculptures, or whirlygigs. One chap planted a ring of daffodils around a huge boulder, deposited by a glacier, at the end of his driveway. You can't see his house from the road, but he announces himself with the daffodil display. A lady in the center of our village planted her entire front yard with crocuses and miniature tulips, for a traffic-stopping show each spring.

I live on a dead-end road so there's not much audience for my gardens. But the delivery people like them, as do the birds and bees.

Decades ago as a young woman, I hiked an old logging track through the mixed fir and hardwoods of the national forest on southern Vermont's Green Mountain Plateau. I was about ten miles from the nearest paved road; except for the singing of birds, it was deeply quiet.

Beaver marshes gave wide views of the summer sky. I ventured off the track. In a sheltered stand of young trees I came upon flowers, ankle-high, that my guidebook called the "small woodland orchis," *Habenaria clavellata*, one of our native wild orchids. The inflorescence was of minute, exquisite white blossoms, rising on a single slender stalk. I was seeing this species for the first time, and there were only a few specimens. In shafts of late afternoon light, I had to lie on my stomach to see the plants well.

What is it about wild orchids that gives them their mystique? Perhaps it's in the flower structure, so architectural, so elaborate, and yet so candid and elemental. Perhaps it's the presentation: the striking flower head rising on the firm slender stem, a kind of floral theater. Or maybe it's that to meet such flowers, we have to exert ourselves, give up civilization, its security and noises, and find our wilder reaches and accept their silences.

When I recall the group of isolated little orchids in their cool, shadowed place, I remember also the wildland quiet and the still-ness in which that floral drama unfolded, as if for me.

I have not been back to that particular spot, and I have not, since then, seen the species, which was likely protected by Vermont law though not necessarily rare. Nonetheless, it was a happy sighting for me. In my memory of that hour in which I met the orchids, I am perennially enraptured, and prostrate on the ground—a posture that is, appropriately, one of reverence, as if I had come a distance to honor a flower in the small sanctum of its wilderness.

Cynthia Locklin / Bennington, Vermont

PUBLIC GARDENS

For Horticulture Deluxe, nothing beats a public garden. Every state in the union has at least one. A favorite of mine is Blithewold Mansion, Gardens, and Arboretum in Bristol, Rhode Island, overlooking Narragansett Bay. In April they host "Daffodil Days," an opportunity to meander through acres of bloom reminiscent of Wordsworth's "host of golden daffodils." And to this day I marvel over a trip, now more than twenty-five years ago, to Hawaii. That entire state is a garden! It's hard to go anywhere un-surrounded by lush and vivid plants. The restaurants even garnish your plate with orchids instead of parsley.

Hawaii, like its climatic opposite, Arizona, offers year-round public gardens instead of the seasonal ones imposed upon other locations. The Arizona-Sonora Desert Museum outside Tucson, for instance, contains a botanical garden, natural history museum, and zoo all in one, all year long. But to catch a full desert bloom anywhere needs fortuitous timing. The bloom comes only after the rainy season, which doesn't occur at all in some years, then inadequately in others. Sometimes all elements blend together just right and the arid world explodes into a magnificent garden. Very, very briefly.

As brief, it seems, as an Alaskan summer. Yet even Alaska has public gardens, such as the Alaska Botanical Garden in Anchorage and the Georgeson Botanical Garden in Fairbanks. These are open during the conventional gardening season of May through September, which is true for much of the country. Some of the larger horticultural organizations, like the New York Botanical Garden in Bronx, New York, are open all year despite being in a four-season climate, as are smaller indoor gardens like the Roger Williams Park Botanical Center in Providence, Rhode Island. Gardens in the South and on the West Coast, of course, enjoy a climate that allows operation 365 days a year.

I'm a pretty mediocre gardener myself, with lots of good ideas but without the accompanying ambition to carry them out. But I do have a recommendation for a terrific public garden in the United States!

Visit the Michigan 4-H Children's Garden on the campus of Michigan State University in East Lansing, Michigan. My daughter was two when the garden was being developed (she's a seventeen-year-old senior now), and her own and a lot of other kids' handprints are embedded in the sidewalk next to the spitting frog fountain. We had an army of parents poised and ready to scoop their kids up from daycares and playgroups and naps and whatever else they were doing the instant the temperature topped forty-five degrees Fahrenheit that early April week when the sidewalks were laid. My daughter was initially afraid to put her hands into the "mud," so her dad and I had to go first before she'd try it. Consequently I think we're the only adults with our hands immortalized in the garden. I *know* she's the only kid with a footprint in it. The garden is next to a railroad track that runs through campus (separated by a large wooden fence with knotholes in it so the kids can see the trains). My daughter was so freaked when a train blew its whistle as she was finally putting her hands into the goo that she jumped about three feet and landed in the cement. The folks supervising the pour decided to leave her footprints there, too.

Our family has spent a lot of hours in the 4-H Children's Garden over the years, touching the sensitive plants to watch them curl up, and investigating the potato roots in the root-view windows. We've maneuvered through the arborvitae maze when the trees were only three feet tall—which was OK because the kids were shorter than the trees were at that point. We've climbed into the wheelchair-accessible tree house to look out over the half-acre garden site with its thirty-three theme gardens artistically arranged across the vast expanse. We've played the step-on-'em chimes from the time the kids were too small and light to make them ring without an adult adding a little heft to now, when no help is necessary, or wanted.

My kids (our son is almost fourteen) are like almost every other kid who has ever visited the garden, whose theme is "please touch!" They regard the garden as *theirs,* and even though they're "too old for some of that little-kid stuff now," they still like to visit and see what's going on in their garden.

It's a great place, and I highly recommend it.

Rebecca McKee / East Lansing, Michigan

Another place I'd like to visit someday is the International Peace Garden: a 2,339-acre botanical garden straddling the U.S.-Canada border in North Dakota and Manitoba. Comprised of ever-changing formal gardens and two fixed floral displays of the American and Canadian flags, it features a bell tower and chapel, as well as memorials for World War II and 9/11 (including steel girders from the fallen World Trade Center). The government of Japan contributed seven Peace Poles bearing the sentiment "May Peace Prevail" in twenty-eight languages. A stone cairn marking the U.S.-Canada boundary—the longest unfortified border in the world—bears this promise: "To God in His glory we two nations dedicate this garden and pledge ourselves that as long as man shall live we will not take up arms against one another."

A comforting thought! And totally appropriate for any garden, which should always be a haven, no matter what its form.

There are too many public gardens to itemize here, so I've included a short list plus books and websites covering them in the Resources. Likewise for full-immersion experiences such as farm vacations and eco-camps. Those have to be planned, but visits to most public gardens can be spontaneous. Organized garden tours do exist, ranging from a given community's annual show-and-tell (usually a fund-raiser) to group vacation tours, including special ones that give access to places the general public can't go and are led by professional botanists.

Recent years have brought garden adventures in the form of canopy tours of the rainforest, involving zip lines and suspension bridges, which allow intimate interaction with trees. For a quieter outing, stop in at any historic home in your own region, for those preserved mansions almost always have lovely grounds.

SIX

The Intangibles

You do not need to know anything about a plant
to know that it is beautiful.

—MONTAGU DON

For the most part, gardens are experienced directly,
whether by your own hand or by passing through them,
observing. That doesn't mean you must engage with plants
physically in order to have them in your life. Indirect experience
counts: looking, learning, thinking, and feeling, and just plain
appreciating. Plants make up such a large percentage of our
world, it's hard to find an area where they don't play a part.

VIRTUAL GARDENS

Books and Videos

Armchair travelers can enjoy plants through print and electronic
media. It does take a bit of legwork to find them, but great books
and videos about plants can be obtained for the effort. Through
them we can visit the grandest gardens of the world, or learn
about cultivating and cooking vegetables. The range is limited

only by what vendors and libraries stock or can be ordered online.

Videos cover everything from seeds to sequoias, rainforest to remedies, ferns to photosynthesis. I adore anything by naturalist Sir David Attenborough, who offers both a book and DVD called *The Private Life of Plants.*

This was a series that ran on BBC television, described (on a mix of British and Australian websites selling the product) as an action film of plants: "Crawling, flying, exploding, thieving, fighting, killing . . . on the move, dangerous and achieving the mission impossible—survival . . . Each program takes one of the major problems of life—growing, finding food, reproduction—and the varied ways plants have evolved to solve it" all around the world.

Wow!

I hadn't thought about plants as such dramatic entities before. But as Attenborough proves, we're all manifestations of the same ingredients and needs, with plants paralleling our lives in slow motion. He points out their evolutionary achievements: colonizing the entire planet, reaching into extremes beyond what any animal can tolerate. Only humankind has the power to wipe them out, which would wipe us out as well.

Makes you think twice . . . which thinking leads, inevitably, to opening one's heart and mind. Consider this: We have absolute power over plants. Ab-so-lute. We can walk on them, eat them, chop them down, rip them up, poison them, ignore them. They can't protest or fight back. But if they go away, we're dead. This shocking fact is hard to grasp when you zip to the supermarket and buy all the food you need. When you think about it, though, and really understand the science involving food chains and atmospheric dynamics, it makes sense.

When I went through that exercise, I was struck dumb by

shame. Plants reminded me of my place in the scheme of things, which is so easy to forget in this day and age. That reminder is what really opened my heart and made me look twice, think twice, feel twice about plant life. I began to evaluate what's really important, and to reprioritize my life.

Writer Michael Pollan examines how society developed its attitudes toward plants in his book *Second Nature,* which is also an engaging tale of his metamorphosis into a gardener. Pollan's and Attenborough's works have hugely influenced my own outlook on gardens by enabling me to see a broader perspective. Plants carry a romantic aura that focuses mainly on their beauty. Looked at through not-rose-colored lenses, however, you see a starker truth. "In gardens, beauty is a by-product. The main business is sex and death," said novelist Sam Llewellyn in his book *The Sea Garden* (Headline Book Publishing, 1999). That's painfully true, because most of the beauty generated by plants evolved as a means of reproducing themselves.

The jarring we feel from trying to reconcile plants' fairy-tale beauty with law-of-the-jungle reality opens our hearts with a crowbar. Once you've become aware of the plant paradox, you can no longer hide your head. Wisdom, peace, and enlightenment—the ideals we seek—come from understanding the universe and our role in it. I received the jolt that brought me to this awareness through Pollan's and Attenborough's works, which are written in awe and wonder. There are many more books and videos out there, similarly toned, that flesh out the floral portrait. Keep questing until you find the work that resonates with you.

Gardens have long lent themselves to coffee-table books as well as guides and journals. A quiet session in one's favorite chair viewing photographs of glorious gardens is almost as good as being there. Some of the seed catalogs show flowers so dense and luscious it's almost impossible to resist the urge to plant your own. (See chapter seven for wisdom about resisting!) You can share other gardeners' experiences through their stories or garner ideas from how-to books and magazines available at any bookstore or library. I don't think there's an aspect of gardening that hasn't been covered in print or on the Web.

Shops and Markets

Once I became aware of plants, I got a little crazy. They are everywhere, just everywhere! In endless form. Obviously, florist shops and nurseries. But the supermarket came as a surprise. Not only is an array of bouquets and potted flowers available, but you can also buy seeds, fertilizers, and potting soil, and sometimes even bulbs while you pick up the milk. Just the other day I was startled to encounter full-size herb plants in the produce section to help people start their own kitchen gardens instead of buying herbs cut or dried. Some metropolitan superstores sell exotic fruits and vegetables from foreign lands as well as locally grown edible flowers such as nasturtiums, and seasonal delicacies like fiddlehead ferns.

Even that bastion of consumerism, the mall, has been invaded by gardens. Between the exterior landscaping and interior atriums, gardens define and decorate that most unnatural of environments. Inside the shops, you still can't escape them. Because plants arrived on Earth before us and we evolved into their world, we've unconsciously carried their image with us in umpteen forms. Browsing through a clothing store reveals floral-print fabrics spanning the continuum from subtle tone-on-tones to multihued extravaganzas. It doesn't end there: tablecloths, curtains, bedding, jewelry, footwear, housewares, upholstery, rugs and carpet, and tapestries. Sewing and craft shops bedazzle the eye with racks of fabric bolts in seemingly infinite floral patterns, from which you can make anything wearable, usable, and decorative for yourself or your home.

If pressed, I would say the simplest thing you can do to bring plants into your life is buy a swatch of cloth that pleases you and set it someplace where you'll see it daily. There's no law that says you can only enjoy living botanicals. Representations serve just as well!

Visual Arts

Artists for millennia have sought to capture plant-life's images and essence. While I have not researched the first appearance of flora in human expression, I do know it occurred a long time ago. In recorded history, artists have conveyed flowers and greenery through portraits and landscapes, some of which hang in the world's top museums: Vincent van Gogh and his sunflowers; Claude Monet and his irises and water lilies. (Monet is credited as saying, "I perhaps owe having become a painter to flowers.")

You can spend hundreds-thousands-millions for original masterpieces or a few bucks for prints and cards by lesser-known individuals. The range of work is so enormous that anyone can find an image that stirs them and install it in their home or workplace. Each time you look at it, you'll experience a moment of pleasure or peace.

I prefer landscapes over flower portraits, but the idea is the same. My mother has a print from a long-forgotten magazine of pretty flowers in a vase, which she likes so much that she framed it years ago. I once visited a crafts fair on a rainy day and was seized by a photograph of lupines that brought back such strong memories and yearnings, I bought the photo on the spot.

It brought to life a sloping field in New Hampshire—acres and acres—of deep purple lupines in full bloom. I had never seen them before. My husband and I were on our way to an event, but at my exclamation of delight he stopped and turned around and we went back to gaze and take photographs. Upon return from this weekend, I looked up the mystery plant and learned its name. Years later, when we moved north, I found that it bloomed copiously in the wild all over our region. I've tried several times to establish a similar population on our property. Haven't succeeded yet, so I look at the photograph to keep the dream alive.

Find an Image

Another image, of Lake Champlain at sunset, doesn't quite qualify as a garden image, but when I first saw it as a greeting card it grabbed me by the throat. I sent that card to my sister, who loves the area but lives far away. Years later, I was still thinking about that image. Needing to see it again, I called her and asked if she still had the card. Yes, she liked it so much she'd kept it around. The publishing credit on the back gave enough artist information to find the work on the Internet. In short order I had a signed print, which I then got framed and now lives over my desk.

Similarly, I was breakfasting not long ago at a local eatery that decorates its walls with offerings from local artists. Over my companion's head hung an image that stirred my soul. Being on a tight budget, I struggled to ignore the painting through the duration of the meal. Finally, on our way up to the cash register, I tipped the frame to see if it concealed a price. Huzzah, the painting was within my budget! So I went out for breakfast and came home with artwork that twangs my heartstrings every day.

Physical Arts

It's hard, once you start thinking about it, to stop counting places where plants intersect with life. So many arts and crafts center on them. Food is the most obvious: Although meat comprises a large part of the American diet, most of the world is kept alive by the vitamins, minerals, starches, proteins, and oils provided by plants. Cooks have always valued fresh spices and produce, both to enhance their creativity in the kitchen and to prepare jellies, jams, preserves, relishes, pickles for the larder. And how many young students have earned favor with teacher by presenting him or her with an apple?

Many artisans depend on plants for their materials. Think of basketry; dried flower arrangements; wreaths and garlands; paint pigments and dyes. Add to that all the woodworking trades, even some masonry (adobe originally was clay mixed with straw), and other manner of housing: straw bale walls, thatched roofs, log homes.

People have long preserved their memories by pressing flowers between pages of a book. This is a great craft for children, popular with parents on rainy days and teachers in the classroom. Same with carving pumpkins, gathering autumn leaves, and sprouting avocado seeds in a jar.

The entire cosmetic industry depends on floral essences and fragrances. Hobbyists use them for homemade soaps and sachets. Florists—professional and amateur—have always used bouquets to brighten or soften a room and convey sentiment. "Say it with flowers" has been a tradition since the 1700s, in which friends and lovers express feelings through blossoms instead of words. A code has developed, assigning meaning to over eight hundred flowers. More than thirty messages are associated with roses alone!

The floral language is called "florigraphy." Best known is the single red rose's message: "I love you." Beware the white rose, however, which traditionally signaled, "I love you not." Over the centuries, the meanings associated with flowers have changed—and, during Victorian times, when sending flowers became a secret language in counter to the restrictions of the era, the language became so subtle that combinations and positions of the leaves and blossoms carried their own subtexts.

Because floral messages can mean anything you want today, it's best to look them up first (see Resources), or include a note for backup. My favorite, the daffodil, can mean either "I do not return your affections" or "The sun is always shining when I'm with you," as well as a few in between. Rosemary, however, seems to have held its meaning: "Never will your memory fade." A great symbol for planting at gravesites.

Messages can come from the lowliest of field flowers, such as the burdock, which communicates, "I refuse to be discouraged" (easy to remember when you try to extract a burdock seed pod from your clothes!). A gift of mullein says, "Let us be friends." If you know someone having a bad day, send them magnolias: "Be not discouraged, better days are coming." And purple loosestrife, currently reviled by ecologists as an invasive plant, has a nobler purpose in settling quarrels: "Take this flower as a peace-offering." Perhaps warring countries should load their bombs with purple loosestrife instead of explosives!

THERAPEUTIC GARDENS

Any form of gardening is therapeutic on an emotional level. Gardens can provide therapy on a physical level as well. As time goes by, more and more garden and medical professionals are addressing the healing aspect of the living green world, to the point where "horticultural therapy" has entered the lexicon.

Horticultural therapy differs from therapeutic horticulture in that it's a formal mode of physical and psychological therapy recognized by the FTC (Federal Trade Commission) since 1973. Therapeutic horticulture is more the everyman's healing system, and is described in "Accessible Gardening for Therapeutic Horticulture" (see below) by Jean Larson, Anne Hancheck, and Paula Vollmar (University of Minnesota, University of Minnesota Extension, 1996, www.extension.umn.edu/garden).

Do you recall times in the garden when, after weeding a row of flowers, you had more energy? Or after a walk outdoors, you felt more peaceful? If so, you experienced the therapeutic benefits of horticulture, and you are one of many who retreat to the garden to relax, renew energy, create a sense of place, and restore self-esteem.

Therapeutic Horticulture is the purposeful use of plants and plant-related activities to promote health and wellness for an individual or group. A garden benefits you on many levels. One seemingly magical effect of gardening is stress relief. Emotional benefits of gardening may derive in part from the sense of the natural rhythm of life that plants and gardens impart. It can divert thoughts about yourself and your situation. In the garden, you can create and control your environment. This control is empowering. Gardening stimulates all of the senses, giving great pleasure and satisfaction. You can design a garden to challenge your strength and balance, or promote eye-hand coordination, range-of-motion, and endurance to just about any degree you want. Cognitively, gardening benefits the mind. Designing a garden and learning about plants and specific gardening techniques can be done in a number of simple or complex ways. And with books or classes, you can learn new things year-round.

There is a growing list of public gardens designed expressly for healing purposes. Some are aimed at children; others at people with disabilities and terminal illness. There are therapeutic gardening programs for prisoners and for the elderly. As well, many botanical gardens have reconfigured their grounds to allow handicap access and/or have created special sensory gardens. A great deal of information about where these gardens are located, and how to design your own, is available on the Internet (see Resources for more information).

My husband and I are in the process of creating a sensory/therapy garden for children with special needs, in response to the passing away of our third child two years ago at age two. The concept for this garden started after Ethan was granted a Make a Wish. Our son Ethan suffered from a severe seizure disorder, which led to many other medical complications. We reflected on what would be an appropriate wish for our child who had many medical needs, had been hospitalized many times, and had a difficult time leaving our home.

He was also a gentle soul who found pleasure in simple things like lying on the grass looking up through the pine trees to the sky, feeling the wind blowing through his hair, and experiencing the sensation of water running through his hand. Together we decided that we would create for him a sensory therapy garden where he could be close to home, but be able to take pleasure in the simple things he enjoyed. Ethan's two big sisters became very excited about planting flowers and creating special garden elements like wind/light catchers for him to enjoy in the garden. Unfortunately, he passed away before we could begin work on his Make a Wish.

After Ethan's passing, our girls asked, "Mommy and Daddy,

Handicap Access

does this mean we won't be able to make the garden?" We assured them that we would try to fulfill this wish as best we could, even though Make a Wish would not be a part of its inception. We decided that we would dedicate the garden to Ethan's memory and invite children with special needs to come and enjoy it as we had hoped Ethan would have. Through the amazing support of family and friends, we were able to begin the realization of Ethan's garden.

In contrast to one's ability to plan and shape a garden, with Ethan's illness we had little control. As we helplessly watched his illness progress and his skills decline, we struggled to make sense out of why this was happening to our beautiful little boy. After many tests and procedures, doctors used words to describe Ethan like "diagnostic conundrum" and "perplexing." The cause of his disorder was never identified.

Our time with Ethan has forever changed us and has taken us down new paths. I was a practicing landscape architect who now works with the Family, Infant and Toddler Program of Vermont, an organization that helps to provide early intervention services for children ages birth to three who have developmental delays or special needs. I am also pursuing certification in horticultural therapy (HT) with the New York Botanical Garden in order to be able

Ethan's Garden

to offer HT programs to children while they visit Ethan's garden. My husband is a landscape architect and city planner by training and currently teaches middle-school language arts. He also serves on the board for the organization for which I now work. We both used our knowledge of landscape architecture and love of gardening to collaborate on the design of the garden. The garden was initiated late in the summer of 2005 and we hope to open it up to the special needs community in the summer of 2008.

My husband spent most of two summers building a long stone wall in the garden that supports a large perennial border at a height that is wheelchair accessible. He found a wonderful catharsis in laying each stone himself while building this beautiful wall. My catharsis comes from digging in the soil, nurturing each plant, and marveling in the wonders of growth. We get such pleasure every day as we walk out in Ethan's garden and see the all the new life there, hear the birds singing, and see our children and their friends playing/smelling flowers/picking vegetables, etc. We can feel our son's presence there.

On Ethan's headstone there is an inscription that reads, "Those who live no more echo still within our thoughts, words and deeds. What they were is woven into what we have become." We truly feel that the changes we have made in our lives can be directly attributed to our experiences with Ethan. As we develop the garden, we can feel that Ethan's sprit echoes within us. Working on the garden has helped to ground us and to make some sense out of everything we went through with Ethan—why he was in our lives and what we learned from him.

Ethan never said a word, but he had his own unique way of communicating. He had the gift of building a community of loving, caring people around him. We believe Ethan's spirit will live on in this garden and continue to touch the visitors who come to enjoy it.

Rachel and Richard Boyers / Essex Junction, Vermont

A verse I have seen all my life—on rocks and plaques in town gardens and country gardens, inside homes and in stores; as a greeting card and poster; and in every collection of quotations in print or online I've browsed through—says it all:

God's Garden

Dorothy Frances Gurney (*Poems*, 1913)

The kiss of the sun for pardon,
The song of the birds for mirth—
One is nearer God's heart in a garden
Than anywhere else on earth.

SEVEN

Green Thumbs and Black Thumbs

My green thumb came only as a result of the mistakes I made
while learning to see things from the plant's point of view.

—H. FRED ALE

For every human endeavor—art, craft, sport, enterprise—
there's someone who seems born to it. In gardening, people we call "green thumbs" have an intuitive sense of plants, and their gardens appear to the rest of us as paradises of effortless cultivation.

Oh, to have that gift!

Yet gardening can be learned, just like anything else. Green thumbs result from experience as much as from gift. Author Michael Pollan, who made this discovery through his own start-from-scratch odyssey, puts it this way in his book *Second Nature:*

"The green thumb is the gardener who can nimbly walk the line between the dangers of over- and undercultivation, between pushing nature too far and giving her too much ground. His garden is a place where her ways and his designs are brought gracefully into alignment. To occupy such a middle ground is not easy—the temptation is always to either take complete control or relinquish it altogether, to invoke your own considerable (but in the end overrated) power or to bend to nature's. The first way is that of the developer, the second that of the 'nature lover.' The green thumb, who will be neither heroic nor romantic, avoids both extremes. He does not try to make water run uphill, but neither does he let it flow wherever it will."

A large portion of green-thumbness comes from the willingness to experiment and to accept failure. "If you are not killing plants, you are not really stretching yourself as a gardener," said J. C. Raulston ("horticulturist extraordinaire" and former director of the North Carolina State University Arboretum, which is now named after him). The patience required to attain this willingness, and be flexible enough to accept Nature's ups and downs, leads to and results from opening one's heart.

Author Barbara Pleasant, in her book *Gardening Essentials,* sums it up neatly in her opening title and subtitle: "How to Garden: Break the rules, keep it simple, have fun. Imagination, persistence and a willingness to be amazed: These are the three characteristics you must have to be a . . . gardener."

The ellipses in that last sentence replace the author's original word: "successful." I deleted it here because these days the word "success" implies achievement (per the dictionary: "the attainment of wealth, favor, or eminence"), which is probably not what the author meant, and definitely not what I wish to imply. "Success" does have a second meaning, now labeled obsolete in the dictionary: outcome, result. Good results come from a green thumb's open and flexible, positive attitude. Great results come when the gardener enjoys Nature's caprice and stays willing to roll with it. Poor results happen to everyone, regardless of their experience level. And for everyone, results will differ every year.

Meanwhile, working the earth provides its own satisfaction. When asked what they like about gardening, many gardeners answer that they like getting their hands dirty. It feels like honest work, especially compared to other things we have to do in life. If nothing else, gardeners get to enjoy the fruits of their own labor in the form of beauty and/or bounty and/or physical fitness and good mental health. I garden in order to attain all facets of this bounty. Non-gardeners often long to experience the same.

Whichever gardening type you are—skilled, novice, wannabe, or "non"—you can bring a garden's benefits into your life. I've passed through all those phases and now consider myself a lazy gardener, meaning, I want the results but with minimal work.

This presents the bottom line of gardening: What is your nature?

All your best intentions will lead to frustration if you work against your own grain. You need to know in your heart, for example, if you want to share. Many folks garden because it allows them to step away from the stresses of their world; they want solitude, and peace, and the simplicity of caring for something real and natural and beautiful that makes no strident demands. A garden, for them, is a sanctuary.

Other folks want gardening to be a communal venture: lots of interaction with helpers and mentors; a setting for parties and games; a food source, or work of art, to share with friends, family, neighbors, coworkers, or hungry strangers. Some folks find spiritual meaning in gardens, as a way to integrate with our mother Earth, or a personal god; they find intimacy with other people through the act of cultivating plants and experiencing the miracle of growth.

Still others enjoy gardening as a competitive sport. Can they grow the biggest pumpkin for the state fair? Can they breed a new variety of rose? Can they win prizes for the exquisiteness of their orchids?

So, what is *your* nature? Your garden is—will be—should be—all about *you*. It might not seem that way if you're gardening to feed a family or earn a living. In those cases, yes, you must consider the tastes and priorities of others. Still, if *you* are the one doing the labor, then it's *your* garden, and *you* get to choose how to do it and should always plant something that *you* want to grow.

There is no right or wrong in a garden. It's all about *your* personal relationship with the living green world.

A New Variety of Rose

I garden because I want some produce. The tomatoes in the grocery store are lousy these days. So I started with tomatoes and have experimented with other vegetable as well. Some work, some don't.

There is some satisfaction from being able to go out into my backyard and pick vegetables to be eaten that day. However, I do not count on anything actually growing. I have had some success with herbs and this is pleasing, as they are expensive and very perishable in the store. There is nothing you can buy that compares to, "I just picked it five minutes ago."

I don't feel bad about wasting food if I am not around to pick or eat it, or if it doesn't get watered enough. I do like to watch it grow. I don't use any fertilizer or anything to repel predators. I don't even wash it before I consume it. I like the idea that I know where it comes from and I don't have to worry (as much) about whether it could make me ill.

It doesn't take much time, luckily, as I am pretty much a plant-it-and-forget-it sort. The minute I find it time consuming and labor intensive, I shall give it up. I travel a lot and don't own any pets; this is probably my substitute dog/cat.

Adrienne Hughes / Spencerport, New York

Gardening is a profoundly basic pastime. The individual tasks are simple, though it takes knowledge and experience to link them up just so in order to get the desired result. So a key concept to grasp is that difference between "simple" and "easy"— two words we often use to describe the same thing.

Our minds relax when gardening because the act is simple. At the same time our minds flourish because they are challenged by the paradox of simple tasks not being easy.

Digging, for example, is not easy. Hauling hoses or watering cans or pots or wheelbarrows around is not easy. Just simple in aspect.

Making selections of what to grow is not easy, because you have to factor in so many conditions. Acquiring tools is not easy, because of the multitude available to choose from that cost money—which you need to earn. And using tools isn't easy if you've never handled them before, or you have chintzy ones that don't work very well.

Finding time is not easy, unless you're free of the need to generate income and have no active family in-house. Caring for what you plant isn't easy, because of weather and bugs and soil and all the things you can't predict or control.

Yet each element, each action, by itself, is simple. I finally understood this paradox during the hay bale episode recounted in chapter three. Such a simple idea, which turned into a time-consuming project to implement that fought back each step of the way! But, once I went through it all, I learned the pitfalls and enjoyed success. So for next year I know how to approach getting, setting up, and cultivating hay bales. And that next time will be easy as well as simple.

A much harder lesson to learn is resisting temptation. The sight of other people's gardens can be inspiring. The photos in garden catalogs can be intoxicating. The assurance given by gurus can be seductive. Like me, you surely envision a grand result from your efforts.

But to all gardeners experienced and raw I counsel, Resist! Resist!

Dreaming too big can overwhelm you with reality. There's a rogue element with plants—and weather—that can set you back no matter what you do. Because the benefits of gardening are gentle, often subtle, and build over time, there's no point in setting yourself up to be crushed on first attempt. The wisest and most difficult course is to take your garden in baby steps.

Prepare, also, to walk your own path. That rogue element I mentioned? It pops up where you least expect it. Gardens demand individuality. And truth, with plants, is relative.

In addition, a garden, once started, requires follow-through in order to avoid disappointment. So if you evaluate your resources before digging in—or step back and reevaluate if you're already underway—you can shorten the learning curve and skip a few setbacks. This is particularly valuable if you live in a region that experiences true winter. Those days below freezing force you to wait many months before you can try again, making it easy to lose momentum. If you embrace gardening as a perpetual growth experience, however, then the dormant season is when you can absorb the events of the summer and start planning for the next round . . . which gives you something to look forward to. And a progressive improvement to reassure yourself with. And a challenge to live up to. All in the privacy of your own backyard!

I garden because I can share. I grow eggplant because it's purple—my favorite color—but also because I can give it away. I garden because I'd rather be outdoors instead of indoors.

My favorite aspect of gardening in winter is mint. Somebody gave me some mint many years ago; knowing that it's invasive, I planted it in an area where I could let it go. One winter while shoveling snow, I accidentally hit one of the plants and got a shovel full of broken leaves—and a waft of mint aroma totally unexpected and delightful for that time of year. Now I look forward to that little surprise, since my mint could be anywhere.

Most of my organized gardening is with vegetables. I grow cherry tomatoes because I can eat them while I harvest them. The best time to eat them is in the morning after a rainstorm, when they are fresh and moist and warmed by the sun . . .

I started with houseplants, since I couldn't outside-garden until I had my own house. I brought home a large jade plant and had to find a place in my parents' house for it. There were no other plants in the house at that time, but that changed! My mother would say, "The farmer skipped a generation" in our family because my grandfather was a farmer and my mother was not, and I was starting to turn into one.

The only reason I do any flowers is the hummingbirds. I love to sit on the deck or in the kitchen with a cup of coffee and watch them. I have been known to be late for work because I've been watching the hummingbirds . . .

Vivianne Majewski /
Litchfield, New Hampshire

True
Winter

If you live in the country, it's easy to come by tools, materials—and space. Progressing closer to the city, they become more complicated and expensive to acquire. All gardeners need the same supplies: gloves, a few hand tools like a trowel and fork, a few larger tools like a shovel and pitchfork, and devices like buckets, watering cans, hoses, wheelbarrows, and pots. Then there is compost, fertilizer, mulch, plant supports, and the plants themselves—seeds, seedlings, shrubs, and trees. It all adds up quickly, especially if purchased in one shot.

You can learn everything you need to know from reading gardening literature and surfing the Internet. (Or working with a mentor.) Conversely, there is so much information out there, and so much of it contradictory, that the road between where you are and where you want to be can prove too intimidating to travel. Another reason to keep your projects bite-sized at first.

Personally, I've about given up on gardening how-to books, even though I continuously add them to my library. Each source has something useful or fascinating to offer. Trouble is, expert advice rarely applies to my personal patch! And plants often don't behave like they're supposed to, even when you do everything right. There will always be a surprise factor. If you factor that factor into your expectations, then you won't get knocked off stride.

GARDENING ABCS

No matter what approach you take, you must work with the three immutable truths about plants: **A.** They need light; **B.** They need water; and **C.** They need nutrients.

Also, they can't take extremes of hot or cold, wet or dry. (While yes, there are some exceptions, they're more esoteric than the material this book covers.)

Within those ABCs, you can create a world. So your main task is to narrow down what you need to know in order to grow the plants you want.

Start with your vision and work backward. Do you want a field of golden daffodils? A perfect rose or bonsai tree? An ever-changing bouquet as a centerpiece for your dining room table? Big, juicy slicing tomatoes? Indoor trailing blossoms year-round? A continuous outdoor bloom all spring-summer-fall? Do you want a yard aflutter with birds and butterflies?

Or all of the above?

The honeysuckle cascading over my fence reminds me of my Missouri grandmother. Red geraniums paired with asparagus ferns transport me to my Iowa grandmother's screened-in porch. And an open Peace rose in a pewter bud vase takes me back to my mother's kitchen table.

I am not a gardener who selects bedding plants to coordinate with the sand-colored brick on my house. The colorful perennial beds in neighbors' yards don't tempt me.

I am a sentimental gardener.

The plants that lure me at open-air nurseries are those that stir memories of several generations of my family who found nourishment and pleasure from digging in the dirt.

I remember kitchen gardens filled with cucumbers for turning into home-canned bread-and-butter pickles, and tomatoes and peppers that often ended up in relish. Hollyhocks, sweet peas, and clumps of black-eyed Susans brightened these practical patches.

As a child, I spent hours playing on my grandmother's front steps flanked by "snowball bushes." I remember by coaxing a thirsty hydrangea through the sweltering Texas summer. Honeysuckle vines on my fence go untrimmed so I can offer my children the food of butterflies. "Pluck a honeysuckle bloom and bite its tiny tip for a taste of sweet nectar," my grandmother taught me.

Miniature water lilies in a half-barrel water garden remind me of my mother's favorite flower. She admired lilies in the backyard pond, but preferred to drop a fishing line among their sunken stems. She grew up on the Mississippi River and was legendary for her ability to catch fish in the river's quiet sloughs.

My azalea bush brings a smile when I think of my dad's determination. He refuses to believe that azaleas are too sensitive for his Midwestern climate. Instead, he treats them as annuals and replants each spring.

I'm trying something new this spring—sweet peas. Their blooms brightened my grandmother's kitchen all summer. I planted the seeds in February, and now they're tall enough to begin climbing the tomato cages I'm using as trellises.

In a few weeks, I'm counting on a bouquet for my kitchen table.

Nancy Lowell George / Richardson, Texas
(This article first appeared in *The Christian Science Monitor,* www.csmonitor.com.)

Whatever your vision, you must reconcile it with your facts of life. If you live in a fourth-story walk-up in the heart of a metropolis, you can forget about the field of golden daffodils—unless you're willing to get involved in community gardening, or join a garden club that manages local parks, or trek out of town routinely to volunteer at a nature preserve. In other words, assess how much time you have available, and of that how much you're willing to commit.

Then think about disposable income. If you're on a tight budget, decide whether you want to scrounge. There are many ways to acquire tools and materials for free, or cheaply, but they involve work and imagination and sometimes a bit of embarrassment. Do you have the time and energy to scout for things—yard sales, the dump, curbside castoffs, dents-and-scratches from garden centers, leftovers from friends and family—then carry them home? If you're able to zip over to the local nursery and load a vehicle with bags of soil, long-handled implements, and flats of plants, then no problem. Likewise if you can afford to have someone haul things to you and do work for you. There's no one way that's right; you need only be frank with yourself. You can find interest and satisfaction with a single potted plant as well as a fifty-acre estate.

Don't overlook physical condition. While gardening does get you into shape and keep you there, it can put a strain on your body parts whether you're fit or not. If you're coming to it cold—either starting a first garden or returning to one after winter—it's easy to overexert without warning and do a number on your back. Or shoulder. Or elbow—I hurt mine by heaving a full watering can out of a rain barrel with one hand.

Learn the proper way to lift and bend, using your legs and abdomen. Do something to maintain your strength during off-season. Ask for help when you need it, and use padded kneelers with handles if you expect to spend long intervals on your knees. Even the healthiest knees get creaky in that situation. Also, be aware that standing up too fast from kneeling or squatting can drain your head too fast and keel you over. By taking it easy and using common sense, your gardening will offer pleasant, low-impact exercise instead of an exhausting marathon.

If you already have an infirmity, spend some time investigating therapeutic gardening and learn what's out there for work-arounds (see Resources).

A final logistic to consider is storage space. You not only need a place to grow your plants, but also a place to stow the related paraphernalia. Some of it can stay outside all year, but other stuff needs protection from weather. And/or thieves, and/or varmints, and/or neighbors with an acute sense of tidiness and propriety. Don't gear up for a garden project without addressing this detail.

Once you've worked out the logistics, you can focus on the ingredients.

A. Sun

Being the photosynthesis factory for our planet, and thus the foundation of the food chain, plants must have sunlight. Fortunately, this imperative is flexible across the plant spectrum, so that many types grow in different lighting. Else anyone who lives near trees would be unable to garden!

If you do have trees, or land with dramatic contour, you can save yourself some grief by prowling your territory for sun patterns before you plant. "Day length," says the USDA on its website, "is usually the most critical factor in regulating vegetative growth, flower initiation and development, and the induction of dormancy." So track the sun until you know how it shines on where you want your garden.

Then plant accordingly—first considering whether that garden will be permanent. Previous owners of our place set up a gorgeous raised bed on the south side of the house thirty years ago. Clearly, they didn't expect trees a few yards away to grow seventy feet tall and put the garden into shade half the day! By the time I arrived, the garden was receiving only four to six hours of direct sunlight. I failed to account for this when I put in tomatoes. Their poor performance made sense after I moved them to deck planters, where they got the eight to twelve hours they require.

By such episodes has my list of *want-to-grows* been reduced to *can-grows*. The restricted sun in our yard, plus the short season that goes with our latitude and the cooler air that goes with our altitude, limits possibilities. But what does grow here thrives, so

I'm learning to build my garden with those flowers, and to employ season-extending tools for my vegetables. If I had done more homework before starting, I could have spared myself much frustration.

B. Water

Where you live will drive your next decision in the time + labor + money + personality equation. Unless you are growing cacti in the desert, you will need to regularly water your plants. Much of the United States is a temperate, four-season climate with rain guaranteed every month. This is enough to keep almost any garden alive. Vegetables and many flowers need more—water every week and in some cases every day—which you have to provide if Nature doesn't. Your garden plans therefore should include time and equipment for watering.

At my place, we use a combination of rain barrels and watering cans, and I'm always trying out different watering aids. My garden is spread out across several acres, and our well is low-volume, which precludes use of a hose. My wallet precludes an automatic irrigation system. So I water by hand—a time-consuming routine that motivates me to redesign my gardens each year in order to reduce the need.

If you live in a compact environment, then a hose and a faucet will serve, especially if you're on city water. If you live in more tropical climes, where it rains almost every day, then your problem is probably too *much* water. (Solve this with raised beds, quick-draining soil, and enough space between plants to let them dry out.)

Many gardeners dress their soil surface with mulch to minimize evaporation. On open land like the plains, wind sucks moisture out of foliage as well, creating the need to water daily regardless of mulch. Aside from retaining moisture, mulch reduces weed growth and creates a tidy visual effect. Some gardeners add water retention pellets to the soil as well, while others set up drip planting systems. An effective trick is to take plastic jugs (milk or orange juice containers) and punch a few small holes in the bottom. Embed them next to your plants, taking care to avoid injuring roots; fill the jugs with water, then replace their caps. *Voilà,* instant drip watering system. Same idea for a few dollars more: prefabricated drip cones that screw onto conventional soda bottles. The idea shared by all these systems is to get water to the roots and keep it there.

As with sun, individual plants have individual requirements as to how much water they need, how often. Plants you purchase at nurseries or from catalogs should come with this information. If not, look it up. Likewise for the plants that came in your yard or garden. You will also need to increase the attention you pay to the weather forecast, and arrange for your plants to be watered when you're away (or invest in self-watering systems).

My family planted roots in Southern California's thirsty soil generations ago, and the family garden has been a long-standing tradition. My earliest memories as a young girl were working in the garden alongside my parents and grandmother, and I've always loved the rain. On my thirteenth birthday, my grandmother gave me a rain gauge.

Southern California is basically a desert. Rain is almost an event; a rainy day is a day people remember. I suppose if you live in an area of the country that measures annual precipitation by the foot, keeping track of rainfall may not be important. But here, too much or too little rain drives headlines, ranging from "homes sliding off hillsides in Los Angeles" to "greater LA burning."

I started recording daily rainfall the day after my grandmother gave me my first rain gauge, and like the official rain stations, I've been keeping a July 1 to June 30 rain journal ever since. Gaps exist of course, such as when I lived away during college or I've been out of town or there's been pressing family issues. But, for the most part, my records reach back nearly five decades.

My first gauge was a simple vial-on-a-stake-styled gauge made out of glass. Now that I'm on my fifth or sixth gauge, I can say that I prefer glass gauges over the plastic ones. Birds love to perch on the plastic ones; their strong claws tend to crack the plastic easily. And I like the tube to measure at least five inches and be calibrated to the tenth, even hundredth, of an inch. Los Angeles can get up to 5 inches of rain during an eight-hour period. But, during years of drought, like this one, Los Angeles has received only 4.3 inches of rain in the last 365 days. Every drop counts.

Keeping track of rainfall is both fun and practical. When a friend said, "The day I got married, it poured," I can flip through my journal and quickly report exactly how much rain we did get on that special day. I also enjoy comparing what my gauge says versus what the official rain stations, located in downtown Los Angeles and Monrovia, record. I've noticed that if downtown LA gets one inch of rain and Monrovia gets two inches, very likely I'll get one and a half inches. Recently, however, Los Angeles moved its official rain station about six miles away from Dodgers Stadium to a flat area with no hills. Suddenly, I began to get more rain than LA. Rain buffs like me have been questioning Los Angeles statistics since the move.

On rainy days, I take my potted plants out from underneath the eaves and put them along the walkways so they soak up the less-salted-than-tap rainwater. I love walking in the rain and look forward to circling the garden with only my seldom-used umbrella for protection. The rain washes the dust off of the holly bush leaves and the air smells fresh again. Unfortunately, it's also a time when my azalea bushes can get decimated in the middle of their bloom; their delicate blossoms pounded into something that looks like wet toilet paper.

There is a certain discipline and perseverance needed to tend a rain gauge. Maybe that's why my grandmother gave me my first one? I know that keeping a rain record makes me more aware of our climate and how it affects our daily lives.

Carolyn Hill / Los Angeles, California

C. Nutrients

Everything your plant needs to "eat" it gets from the soil. The organic approach provides food through natural ingredients; the inorganic approach provides food through industrially processed fertilizers. Organic gardening is best because it benefits plants and people, and ultimately costs less. Inorganic gardening introduces poisons, directly or as by-products, and increases costs over time.

Put your plants in good, clean soil and enrich it by using natural products, of which compost is the most important. If you don't have the space to build your own compost pile, then buy compost from nurseries or fetch it (usually for free) from the municipal dump. Mother Nature creates compost by letting greenery decay into dark, moist, loose soil loaded with earthworms. Anything you can do to emulate the process will help your garden thrive. An entire book has been written about it, called *Weedless Gardening* by Lee Reich. There are also dozens of books out there just about building compost.

The simplest system is to heap all your yard waste and non-animal kitchen waste into a pile, preferably in the sun. Eventually it will break down into nutritious black stuff. You can speed up the chemical reaction by turning the pile; adding commercial ingredients designed to accelerate breakdown; enclosing it in black plastic; and alternating green, moist materials with brown or yellow, dry materials. A popular trick is to fill a black plastic garbage bag with chopped leaves you've raked up during autumn. Close the bag and leave it in the sun over the winter, then spread the rotted leaves on your garden in the spring.

Regardless of what soil your garden contains to start with, you can improve it by adding combinations of the gardener's triumvirate: sand, compost, and peat moss. Dry, sandy soil needs compost and peat moss to give it body and moisture retention. Wet, sloppy soil needs sand and peat moss to give body while drying it out. Dense, clayey soil needs sand, peat moss, and compost to let both air and water penetrate. What you want to end up with is soil that is soft and dry enough to crumble in your hand while moist enough to leave some residue on your hands. Such dirt will, simultaneously, allow water to trickle through and be absorbed by thirsty roots while providing the oxygen and nitrogen plants need in order to thrive.

I'm a landscaper by default. When I switched careers from engineering to horticulture, I wanted to do environmental restoration work. In the early 1990s, the field was generally unexplored and perceived as unnecessary in northern New England. Since there was no real market for that at the time, I moved into sustainable gardening. That's a combination of form and function together—not just form—to make a garden work on its own.

The key is to understand what you're working with. If you don't know what kinds of plants you have, then get a book to tell you. You get exactly what you put in, so don't cut corners. Soil, especially, will reward you tenfold.

When designing a plantscape, use common sense—and build in an expectation of surprise. Plants respond to their environment just like we do. If it works, keep doing it. If not, try something different. Sometimes plants die for no reason. If that happens, think of the great spot—or pot—to put something new in!

I like being a steward of the land. And I enjoy working with something that's living and something that's beautiful. It's a spiritual connection rather than a control connection. I have control only of where they go.

Joan Lynch / Pittsford, Vermont

Plants in containers are walled off from the chemical and organism dynamics that exist in the ground, so they need a more contrived environment. Garden soil tends to compact when potted, necessitating a lighter, more porous mix. Myriad bagged mixes are available at any garden center. You can also make your own potting soil with a roughly equal mixture of peat moss, compost (be it your own, or a blended mix of commercial compost, or composted cow manure), and vermiculite.

Dealing With Dirt is a critical decision point in your time + labor + money + personality equation. If you are blessed with a yard of terrific soil, then all you need to do is plant, water, and wait. Most of us have to help things along a little. And that means an expenditure of work and dollars.

A helpful step I have never taken is getting your soil tested. Whether you hire someone to do it or use one of the handy-dandy kits available from garden suppliers, you will learn the general makeup of your soil and what supplements it needs. The dominant element is pH—the degree of alkalinity or acidity measured on a scale based on a neutral point of 7.0. Below pH 7.0 is considered acidic; above pH 7.0 is considered alkaline.

The pH factor determines how well a plant's roots can draw water and nutrients from the soil. You don't have to pinpoint the pH to three-decimal-point accuracy, since plants by necessity can tolerate a range. But if your soil is way off, so will be your plants.

You can skip the test if you can identify the weeds that grow in your soil. They will tell you what you need to know in broad terms. For example, if your soil gives home to large populations of both dandelion and common mullein, then you're looking at an acidic condition. Healthy populations of campion, stinkweed, nodding thistle, and field peppergrass indicate alkaline soil. Likewise, weeds can signal compacted soil—look for chicory and bindweed—or soggy soils: look for dock, horsetail, oxeye daisy, goldenrod, joe-pye weed. These clues point toward solutions, such as adding lime or wood ashes to neutralize acidity, or peat moss and compost to counter alkalinity.

Weeds benefit your garden in other ways, so don't be overzealous about eradicating them. They reduce erosion; their roots help loosen up the soil and bring deep nutrients to the surface for your crops to use; they attract beneficial insects to aid the garden, or give pests something else to chew on besides your flowers and vegetables.

A healthy soil provides all the nutrients your plants might need. When you do need to add fertilizer, the main ingredients to consider are nitrogen, phosphorous, and potassium. These are indicated on fertilizer packaging as an N-P-K number, e.g., ten-ten-ten for a balanced blend, or seven-nine-five (etc.) for a targeted application.

Nitrogen aids aboveground foliage, enabling plants to grow tall and sturdy with glossy green leaves and stems. Phosphorous helps roots grow strong and flowers and fruits to develop, as well as gives greater resistance to disease. Potassium (potash) contributes to vigor in the form of disease resistance and resilience to weather extremes. Plants also need a host of trace nutrients, which both commercial and organic fertilizers supply in any given blend.

Soil testing provides a baseline that helps you figure out what your garden needs. Without it, you must work by trial and error. The choice, as always, depends on you. Learning your soil's characteristics by observation alone might take several seasons to achieve what could be done in one season with testing, though the experience might teach you more than you'd learn by doing it "right" in the first place. It all depends on your interest in chemistry (or is that alchemy?).

My first recollection of gardening is planting pansies with my mother when I was probably four years old. We lived in a big old house on Long Island, New York, and my mother was, and still is at ninety-four, an avid gardener. Settling in Vermont after college, I realized the potential in growing our own food and began the process of learning how to live off the earth in my own backyard. Through many successes and failures we grew and ate the majority of our veggies during both summer and winter. Our children were raised with the knowledge of where their fresh veggies came from and what it entails to grow a red tomato.

Years passed, kids became adults, pets died, new pets were adopted, and still I was in the garden, and the garden became my life and my work. I first owned an herb business, which evolved into herb display beds, which evolved into weekly garden articles in the local paper (twelve years' worth), which evolved into a garden design business, which matured into being the designer for my son's landscape company. Just as a garden starts with small seeds, my love of the garden started with a small plot and evolved into my life's work and my daily pleasure.

I am consoled by the feel of the earth in my hands when the news of the world is bleak. I am amazed every fall by the gathering of gigantic squashes that have grown from seeds no more than a half inch in length. I am in heaven when weeding and reorganizing my herb and perennial plot by the back door. The scents are overwhelming as I pull out mints-gone-wild, thymes-gone-astray, oreganos whose flowers are loaded with bees as they gather pollen. Hollyhocks grow in rocky crevices where no seed should be able to germinate, and lavenders lash out at me and assault my clothing with their scent as I crawl by on hands and knees. Rue beckons as its seed pods need clipping (but only when wearing gloves, because the oils from the leaves are pungent and rash-inducing).

Plants that have been around for centuries with names like love-in-a-mist, wolfsbane, foxglove (or folks gloves if you look at the shape of the interior petal markings), belladonna (the beautiful, poisonous lady of lure and Shakespearian tragedies), larkspur, horehound, and good-king-Henry—all are plants that still overrun our gardens, cure diseases, season food, and kill unwitting prey.

I am a Master Gardener, a designer by degree, a lover of color, texture, scent, and haphazard organization. The garden is an ongoing challenge because it is a growing medium that is in fluctuating states of life and death, running astray when it should be stationary and being stationary when it should be running astray. No two years in a garden are the same even though the garden plot and plants are the same. No other challenge in life would keep me coming back for more failure and success. Garden plots are my canvas and I try to have the paintings always beautiful, if ever changing, and certainly never boring. Love the earth, feed it with healthy food and it will return the bounty to you in various ways.

Nancy Rowe / Sudbury, Vermont

D. None of the Above

Getting the ABCs in balance leads to a happy garden. Keep in mind that each species requires its own combo of A, B, and C. Adding water or nutrients won't compensate for lack of sunlight, and vice versa. You must work with your plants to either get the right ones into the right environments, or create and sustain the environment(s) they need.

The ABCs can be bypassed by gardening with wildflowers. For this you just need to allot a corner of your land to lie undisturbed. Mother Nature will fill it with every weed you would otherwise be trying to remove from your garden, most of which flower profusely and multiply into dense stands. Your job then is to maintain a contrast—lawn, wall, pathway—against which the wild garden can display itself, and to periodically pull out elements you don't want, such as trees growing into a meadow or one of the various climbers that smother other plants if left unrestrained.

A wild garden will attract birds and butterflies and insects good and nasty, along with four-legged creatures seeking shelter and food. It will showcase the region's native plants and probably grow more lushly than your cultivated patch. Commonly, gardeners will cultivate one corner of their yard and leave another one to run wild for the combined effect.

Ecologically concerned gardeners will go a step further and plant wildflowers that specifically attract pollinators. Members of Monarch Watch, an organization that arose out of the University of Kansas, have created a "way station" program to support Monarch butterflies on their annual migration from Mexico to Canada and back. Nobody knows why Monarchs, alone among tropical butterflies, make this trek that consumes several generations, or how the next generation is born en route knowing how to get back. Regardless, they need nectar plants for food and milkweeds for their eggs and caterpillars, all the way. Gardeners providing way stations replace habitat rapidly being lost to development and herbicides. In fact, home gardens are replacing habitat for all wildlife. Leaving yard and roadside patches to grow wild is something anyone can do to help save the planet.

EIGHT

Nuts and Bolts

The highest reward for a person's toil is not what they get for it,
but what they become by it.

—JOHN RUSKIN

"Impedimenta"

The above is a fancy word for "stuff." Literally, appurtenances, equipment, accessory objects. As touched on earlier, gardening requires tools and supplies, proportionate to the scope of your endeavor. Of these, the most important, in my opinion, is gloves.

Getting one's hands dirty is, indeed, one of the primal satisfactions of gardening. You can achieve this either by digging in directly or by wearing gloves (which don't fully keep your hands clean—quite a bit of dirt gets through the fabric or trickles in around the cuffs). I started out bare-handed but eventually gave in to gloves for practical reasons. First I got a mysterious rash. Then I got tired of scraping underneath my fingernails to clean them, and needing hand lotion more often, and getting lots of small cuts. Nowadays, when I need to do fine work with seeds and seedlings, or picking or tying, I pull off the gloves because even the best are clumsier than naked fingertips. But gloves do protect your skin from unpleasantness like poison ivy, and as I recently learned, from more lethal germs that live in the soil, such as the bacteria that cause tetanus. So if you're not up to date on your boosters, pause and consider before you get into the bare-handed habit.

The light cotton gloves available in any garden store, hardware store, or outdoor section in a department store serve just fine for most applications. I used these gloves for years, until I got tired of the middle two fingers on the right-hand glove wearing out by midseason. That moved me to buy a more durable style with reinforced palms and fingertips. Over time I accumulated a glove for every purpose: rubbery ones for wet work, leather ones for heavy work, mesh ones with leather palms and tips for hot-weather work, cotton ones for light work, long-gauntlet leather-palmed ones for scratchy brush work, and so forth. As I exhaust each pair, I replace it with one of brighter color. Among the many lessons I've learned the hard way is that gloves and tools disappear in a garden unless they are neon colored.

The tool no gardener can live without is a trowel. Anything beyond that is gravy. I expanded into tools as I did gloves, driven by exasperation when my projects demanded more oomph than I was equipped for. I now have quite the arsenal and am almost at the bottom of my list of desired accessories. Each year, though, I undertake something new that asks for a new item to go with it. Yet I use a trowel more often than any tool, matched only by snippers.

The final must-have is a container (or conduit) for watering. A recycled milk jug works for indoor gardening, though a lightweight watering can with a long spout works better. For outdoor gardening, a conventional watering can with removable sprinkler head puts water where you want it without muss or fuss. Nothing beats a built-in irrigation system, of course, but absent that, you can accomplish a lot with very little. The Square Foot Gardening method, for example, is designed to be not only ultra-simple but also to use minimal tools: trowel, and pail with cup.

Pests and Disease

Bugs are everywhere. They will always be there. If you are lucky, and practice good garden hygiene, they will coexist with you and the other denizens of your ecosystem. If you are unlucky, they will wipe out a crop and come back to haunt you next year.

A bug infestation, however, does not have to shut down your gardening. There are many ways to deter or vanquish insects—enough to fill their own book (see Resources). The best solution is prevention, such as choosing disease-resistant, diverse plant varieties; keeping the garden clean, and providing diverse habitats to attract bugs, birds, and bats that eat the undesirables. The majority of insects are either benign or beneficial, so a garden that lets the good bugs dominate stays healthier than one treated with pesticides, which usually wipe out everything in order to get rid of a few.

What might actually shut down your gardening is what bugs do to *you*, not the plants! Who among us likes being bitten and stung, or orbited by buzzing flies? And it seems that bugs are worst at both ends of the summer, when you're out there most, planting and harvesting. I hate wearing stinky repellents on my skin, so often plan my longer sessions to end with a shower—or spray my clothes and dump them into the laundry when I come in. Keep in mind that entering the garden fully perfumed from your favorite shampoo, deodorant, and skin lotion will make the bugs think you're a big flower. ("Don't wear perfume in the garden—unless you want to be pollinated by bees," said Anne Raver, a garden writer.)

Some people say that insects are attracted by dark clothing. What seems like a good solution is the mesh over-clothes I recently saw in a fishing catalog. They're made from mosquito netting, fine-mesh enough to keep out even no-see-ums. That would allow wearing shorts and a tank top on hot sunny days! I'm ordering a set for next year—I don't care how silly I look in my own garden. The outfit will work great for canoeing and hiking, too.

It was the fire ants that did me in.

Without issuing an official declaration, the little Nazis moved into my yard and started taking over everything: my flower beds, garden plot—whatever I regarded as my territory, they decided was theirs. They built mounds with underground tunnel networks and came out fighting if I tried to reclaim my space. During the day, I took my shovel and knocked mounds down. Late at night, I poured boiling water on remaining mounds. I did anything that would be harmful to them but not to the environment. The mounds might go down for a day, but they would be rebuilt in another part of the yard. Their tunnels went a long way. I once went to pull weeds growing in the sandy spaces of my brick walkway, and many soldiers came out quickly, stinging my feet and hands. So I gave up.

I bid my yard good luck, and moved my vegetable garden to my deck. I figured I could garden in containers. Several well-meaning people told me I couldn't grow much in a container. Herbs, mainly, and tomatoes, they said. I planted an herb garden and, oh what the hell, string beans—the purple variety that turn green when you cook them.

Initially, I missed the expanse of my yard garden. I missed getting on my knees and working in the dirt. Naturally, I didn't miss the ants, and I certainly didn't miss the weeds. There were hardly any. The few that made their way in through airborne seeds I was able to remove quickly.

Everything grew just fine in my containers. I hauled an old potting bench to the deck and set the containers on them. Waist-high now, they made it easy to harvest the beans when they were ready. I would go out when I was preparing dinner and pick beans for the meal. From the container to the stir-fry in minutes. Emboldened by my success, I added cayenne pepper plants. They thrived. That fall, I sewed together a long string of cayenne peppers and hung them in the kitchen to dry. It was a nice reminder that I had beaten the ants.

It's been many years since I started a garden on my deck. Now I grow squash, corn, peppers, tomatoes, lettuce, collards, herbs, and more in pots. Only once did I have an issue with ants, and that was because I used soil from my yard that turned out to have a few soldiers. They built a clandestine fort. I found it. Overthrew it. No more ants.

Good.

Barbara Merchant / Covington, Georgia

Research has shown that insects prefer to eat undernourished plants. In *Secrets of Companion Planting for Successful Gardening,* author Louise Riotte adds, "Organically-grown vegetables produced on balanced, healthy soils have significantly lower levels of free amino acids in their tissues than plants grown where chemical fertilizers have destroyed the balance. Such 'organic' vegetables are less tasty to insects."

Companion planting helps draw beneficial insects as well as repel the harmful ones. Certain plants have mutually beneficial relationships with each other, such as basil, which interacts with tomato plants in a way that enhances the tomato's flavor, meanwhile discouraging tomato enemies like hornworms, asparagus beetles, and aphids. Flies and mosquitoes avoid it as well.

Garlic, known for its healthy properties for humans, serves the plant world, too, often interplanted with tomatoes or roses, and around the base of fruit trees. All plants of the allium family, however—garlic, onions, and their ilk—are hostile to beans and peas, so keep them apart. Garlic oil is an effective insecticide against some of the most annoying and destructive insects: mosquitoes, Japanese beetles, spider mites, and aphids. Chives, a relative, is good planted at the base of bird feeders to offend squirrels.

Bee balm not only makes a colorful display in any garden, but also attracts bees, hummingbirds, and butterflies while deterring hornworms and, like basil, aiding flavor and growth of tomatoes. Carrots work both ways, good with tomatoes, lettuce, onions, radishes, rosemary, and sage, and helped in turn by the alliums and herbs which shoo away the carrot fly.

Corn, beans, and squash form the ancient "Three Sisters" of Native American culture. In this symbiosis, corn serves as the poles for climbing beans, which help fix nitrogen in the soil for the corn. At their base romps the squash, covering the soil and retaining moisture while its prickly stems turn away raccoons.

Popular annuals such as geranium, nasturtium, marigold, and petunia, and favorite herbs such as basil, garlic, lavender, mint, rosemary, sage, and thyme, repel a host of insects. Planting them liberally around the garden sends the message and helps keep things under control.

If a problem does arise, responsible gardeners always start with the simplest, lowest-impact solution, then work their way up as crisis demands. Some bugs and grubs can be plucked off by hand and stomped on, or dropped in soapy or salty water. In other instances, nontoxic oils and soaps can be concocted in the kitchen and sprayed on the foliage; sometimes just a blast from a hose clears off the pests.

When a specific insect overruns your garden, zap it with a botanical pesticide. Rotenone and pyrethrum are derived from plants and pack quite a punch without harming mammals, then break down relatively quickly in the environment. Only use synthetic pesticides if you absolutely have to. In small gardens, it's probably not worth it. Better to yank out the plant(s) and try again next year.

My rule of thumb is: If dire circumstances move you to use any sort of pesticide, *read the label first!* Many, if not most, commercial products might solve your pest problem but also take out innocent bystanders, like bees, birds, fish, animals—and you, if you don't use it correctly. Some gardeners avoid the whole dilemma by planting "trap crops" or simply planting more of everything than they need, and letting varmints take the rest.

Varmints come in all sizes and species. As with everything else in gardening, it depends on where you live. Here in the northern boonies, I have remarkably few pests to deal with. Worst experience was a plague of aphids that murdered a stand of lupines. Just those plants, just that year. But every year I get Japanese beetles. I tried traps but that just drew in more—and they reproduced so rampantly that my lawn became infested with their grubs, and therefore moles. That led to treating the lawn with milky spore disease, which specifically attacks Japanese beetle grubs and harms nothing else. I used the slow-uptake powder that needs a few years to be fully effective. Or so the label says. Not enough time has passed to determine the truth. In the meantime, another season of flattening mole hills and plucking beetles off the beans has come and gone.

So much wilderness still stands in these parts that the deer and bears and raccoons and skunks and groundhogs all have other places to browse besides my garden. Nevertheless, each time I turn up dirt, whether placing out a freshened container in the spring or constructing a new garden bed in the fall, some night creature makes a point to dig through it and assure itself that nothing's in there. When a plant does go in, I must add covers or fencing.

In suburbia, lost habitat is pressing wildlife into people's backyards. Manual barriers work the best—wire screen cages, fences, floating row covers—though there are many scent and sound deterrents. Variations of them work for cats and dogs as well. Explore garden catalogs and websites for options germane to your situation.

Don't forget two-legged pests—people who tromp through your garden or help themselves to your flowers and food. Unfortunately, the law disallows solving those problems by discharging a load of buckshot into the culprit's derriere, or bombarding him (or her) with rotten eggs and tomatoes. Let the plants do it for you: Try thorny shrubs like rose and holly, and a barrier of stinging nettles if your garden borders a public way.

To keep those beautiful but hungry deer from eating your flowers and veggies, here are a few easy deterrents passed on to me by a neighbor. They're all simple, inexpensive, and require no power tools.

The easiest method is to simply move things around in your yard. Deer may be made to feel uncomfortable when the surroundings change, perhaps thinking that people are about. Keep a wheelbarrow around and move it from place to place every couple of days. Do the same with lawn chairs, buckets, or whatever else you have on hand. I used this method in conjunction with the next two.

For specific areas such as vegetable gardens, try an easy-to-install fence. First, pound posts into the ground surrounding the garden, leaving enough room for you to easily move around the garden to weed, bring in water, etc., and far enough away from the garden so deer cannot stand outside the fence and reach your plants. My fence was about three feet from the garden's edge. The posts don't have to be particularly sturdy or high; I used one-by-two scraps that were roughly three feet long and sharpened one end to make it easier to hammer them into the ground. Keep one unsharpened post aside. Next, measure the circumference of the posts and cut a flexible mesh fencing to about a foot longer than the circumference. I used a black plastic mesh with half-inch square holes, but you could use a variety of other materials (chicken wire, snow fencing, etc.). Starting at one corner, attach the mesh fence to the posts (I used a staple gun for this). Attach the very end of your mesh fencing to the extra post, making a gate that you can easily open and close. I didn't lose a single thing to deer after I installed this kind of fence around my vegetable garden.

For flower gardens that you do not wish to impair the viewing of or for gardens directly adjacent to your home, try this easy fix: Install a row of short, see-through garden edging roughly twelve to eighteen inches from the beds. You can use scallop-topped plastic-coated wire edging, plastic faux-fence edging, or whatever else suits your fancy. I'm talking *easy* installation here—use the kind of edging that has bottoms that you just poke into the ground. If you're thinking, 'there's no way that will stop *my* deer from munching my flower buds,' think again. Deer apparently don't like to feel constrained in any way. It makes them feel nervous. The fact that they have to step *over* a barrier, even as flimsy a barrier as we're talking about here, should make them nervous enough that those buds in the forest (or in your neighbor's garden) look a whole lot more attractive to them.

These three simple methods, especially when used in conjunction, should protect your blooms and vegetables for years to come. Plus, you get the added bonus of knowing you've outsmarted your neighborhood deer!

Laurie Fila / Germantown, New York

Along with pesky critters, the gardener must occasionally deal with plant diseases. This subject, too, warrants its own volume so I won't get into it here (see Resources for starting points). Some diseases can be easily identified and respond to straightforward treatments. Others are mysterious, like the black spots that keep coming on my tomatoes after they have ripened. Surely a garden expert somewhere knows what those are; I, however, after much reading of descriptions and comparing of pictures and inquiring at nurseries, have yet to discover the cause and therefore the solution. So far, only my hay bale tomatoes have come to fruit without being infected. But the yard garden and all my containers, even though I rotate each year and plant different varieties, keep generating tomatoes that get black spots.

Diseases, like insect invasions, usually go through cycles and usually can be prevented by good management techniques. They also come and go with weather. One spring it was so cold and wet, the wild fruits and berries didn't get pollinated so there was no harvest for the wildlife, and all my tomatoes (yep—tomatoes again!) acquired some sort of black mold on their leaves. You just plain never know what's going to happen in a garden, which is part of the challenge. Nature won't let us take anything for granted!

Basic Plant Info

You can make anything grow if you put enough work into it. However, recreational and therapeutic gardening shouldn't be that tough (unless challenge is what turns you on). Most of us start with the easy keepers like marigolds and hostas, and the three Ds: daffodils, daylilies, and daisies. All are beautiful, bloom at different times, bloom for a long time, and grow in different combinations of sun and shade in most regions.

Buying plants from a local nursery gives best chance for success in your own yard. Catalogs offer a broader range of choice but also higher risk of unpleasant surprise. Local nursery owners will stock what they know survives in the region, both seasonally and year-round. Usually somebody who works there can answer your questions, and some nurseries offer classes.

Make sure you leave enough space between plants. Don't plant too close unless you have very fertile soil or are prepared to fertilize a lot, or else you'll be disappointed in the results, and that's not a good reason to not come back the next year and try again . . . And don't put your bird feeders near the vegetable garden!

Vivianne Majewski / Litchfield, New Hampshire

All garden plants fall into three categories:

❀ *Annuals* provide fast results and easy mass color from spring until fall. Their life cycle—seed to seed—occurs within one year, so they must be planted anew every spring or allowed to run to seed in the garden and launch the next generation. Common annuals: impatiens, marigolds, petunias, morning glories, nasturtiums, cosmos, zinnias.

❀ *Perennials* live for three years or more. They may or may not bloom the first year but then come back and spread in following seasons. The root system stays alive all year long then the upper plant regrows during summer. Some retain their foliage year-round. The gardener's advantage in perennials—only having to plant once—is counterbalanced by a shorter bloom time and periodic need for maintenance and division. Common perennials: daylily, bleeding heart, phlox, oxeye daisy, purple coneflower, chrysanthemum, rose, delphinium, oriental poppy.

Many plants can be classified as annual or perennial, depending on where they are being grown. Flowers such as petunias and geraniums, and vegetables such as tomatoes and peppers, are perennials in their warm native climates. But because they can't survive northern winters, up here they must be annuals.

Biennials take two years to go through their life cycle, and generally bloom in the second year. Common biennials: foxglove, hollyhocks, lunaria, Canterbury bells, sweet William, money plant, evening primrose, forget-me-not, viola, and some herbs and vegetables (e.g., parsley, and carrot if not harvested).

Lilies taught me to be a better gardener.
There are over one hundred seventy-five flowers called lily, but it is the "true" lilies that I discuss.
So, you say, "What is a 'true' lily?"
To mention a few things:
The bulb does not have a protective covering.
It is never dormant.
It needs to be treated as a perennial plant.
Flowers must have six sepals and six anthers.
They are of the genus *Lilium*, a division of the family Liliaceae.

They are the prima donnas of flowers:
    Unique, perfect, enchanting,
Wild, beautiful, different,
    Unpredictable, mysterious, pure.

They are originally from the mountains of:
        Asia, Tibet, India,
        Europe, Africa, Persia,
        The Philippines, and others.

They were used by the ancients for food and medicine;
        carried by the Crusaders to various countries.
        carried by nomadic people.
        used as religious symbols.
        used as a fertility symbol to the goddesses.
        used as a symbol of worship to Mary.
        written about in the Talmud and the Bible.
        carved in Egyptian hieroglyphics.
        placed in the sarcophagi of rulers for food.
        used in the Temple of Solomon.
        used by the rulers of China, Japan and the Popes.
        subject of a real boom of Easter lilies in Bandon,
          Oregon, starting in 1942.

Lilies will give you their best blooms if you give them the bed of
    their choice.
Once settled in their new home, they ask little of you, mostly to
    be left alone with a drink of water now and then.

However, they can be fussy.

They do not like to be treated like other bulbs.
    They like clean, weed-free soil.
    They dislike invasion by other plants, as they often carry
harmful bacteria.

They are more disease-resistant, due to improved hybridizing techniques.

At one stage in their life, lilies can be so fragile the gentlest touch can snap the new sprouts, while at the other end of their life, their tough stalks must sometimes be cut with loppers or a saw.

Yes, there are blossoms without fragrance.
Yes, there are varieties without bothersome pollen.
If your cutting has unopened buds, for days you can watch
    the magic of the unfolding in their time.

I'm certain I'm in Paradise when our home is perfumed with their fragrance,
    when our home is a gallery of color.

Lilies taught me;
    racing against slugs,
    ancient history,
    colors I could not imagine,
    fragrances enjoyable beyond description,
    artistic design from the Great Artist,
    patience and relaxation from the Great Therapist,
    to be a better gardener and a better person.

Liliaceously always.

Eleanor Crick / Portland, Oregon

Gardening itself is the practice of *horticulture* as compared to *agriculture,* which is the cultivation of fields instead of plots. (This distinction gets fuzzy in large-scale vegetable operations, but for the layperson's purposes, horticulture means gardening and agriculture means farming.)

Orchards fall under the horticulture banner, though tree farming is called *silviculture*. The difference comes from what's being grown: fruit versus forest. Vineyards get their own term: *viticulture*, the cultivation of grapes, primarily for making wine.

Herb gardening also falls under horticulture. Within it comes a distinction between who does what. Someone who grows herbs in general is called an "herbarist" while someone who treats people with medicinal herbs is called an "herbalist." One letter difference between them makes a big difference in meaning!

Microclimates

Just as one letter changes the meaning of a word, one foot of distance can change the fate of your plants. If you already garden, then you've surely experienced the hair-pulling frustration of one plant doing well here, then faring poorly over there. Or seen two plants in the same crop row, from the same seed packet or transplant set, behave like different species. Perhaps your neighbor planted the same flowers you did, at the same time, using the same gardening method, and went through the same weather, yet got dramatically different results. Huh? How can things turn out so disparately when all other factors are equal?

Genetics might have something to do with it. Just as children from the same two parents always come out differently, plants from the same stock will vary, too. Commercial breeders of both plants and animals do their best to manage variables and produce consistent offspring. However, it's a sure bet that any batch of seeds will generate diverse individuals.

Beyond that come the variables you introduce while preparing and caring for your garden. But above and below the garden, within and around it, enter the wildcard variables called microclimates.

Microclimates influence every garden, and can drive you bananas if you aren't prepared. Small differences in altitude, soil content, water table, sun and shadow, insect types and life cycles, the presence or absence of bedrock, past land use, wind frequency and intensity—all can affect your plants for better or worse.

In my yard, the microclimates are so small and numerous I call them "nanoclimates." The land undulates vigorously; the water table goes up and down in contrary undulations; tree and shrub stands—both deciduous and evergreen—alternate with untended fields and mowed lawns; air currents swirl in unpredictable directions. On more than one occasion it has rained (or snowed) in the front yard as the sun shone in back. Likewise, frost might fall on one side of the house and not the other, then flip-flop the next day. The soil under all this ranges from rich muck to entire hills composed of sand. And the only sunny spots good for gardening lie beyond reach of a hose.

Such variation occurs everywhere, not just in northern New England. The mountain West and desert Southwest experience sharp extremes of hot/cold, wet/dry, while other regions suffer conditions consistent with their own terrain. Microclimates exist wherever the land changes shape, and buildings or trees block the sun for any part of a day, and water runs near the surface or far below, through different rock and soil deposits.

My pink garden phlox illustrate microclimates nicely. Our house has changed hands many times over its hundred-fifty-year life; three or four owners ago, somebody laid out a perennial bed in what is now an impenetrable thicket. I didn't realize this until I spotted something pink and delicate peeking through the greenery the summer after we moved in. Gee, what's that?

I waded in to find five scraggly phlox—each maybe a foot tall, with a handful of blossoms. I marked them with string then, in the fall, transplanted them to a sunny bed on the opposite side of the house. The next summer they grew to five masses of brilliant pink as tall as I am. By the second summer they had taken over half the garden. The third summer they had taken over the entire garden and pushed out other flowers! Now I dig out half of them each spring and autumn, and still they overrun the bed. If they weren't so beautiful, I would go after them with a blowtorch or a backhoe. Instead, I call them Vermont kudzu and do my best to cope.

But the overflow I've transplanted around the yard have fared differently. They range from scrawny sticks like the originals to all points on the scale between those and the kudzu-like success. These transplants lie within a few yards to a few hundred feet of each other. Each clump sits in different soil, gets different sunlight, accompanies different plants.

In a similar accidental experiment, I relocated a mature stand of shrub hydrangeas. They were established in a very sunny, very protected hill-bottom beside one of our outbuildings, and stood in the way of expansion so had to go. Spouse kindly cranked up the tractor and dug them out with a backhoe, then trundled them around the property, dropping chunks off in different corners at my direction. Like the phlox, they ended up in diverse growing environments. Some barely survived, some did OK, some I'm still wondering about, and one took off explosively. But guess what? The successful one thrives now in almost full shade, on the exposed northwest side of the yard where the weather comes from. Completely opposite from the environment it started in. Huh?

Then there's the Russian sage, but we won't go there. Suffice it to say, that plant is what taught me the difference between books, zone maps, and reality.

Zone Maps

To get an idea what gardening climate you live in, consult the USDA Plant Hardiness Zone Map. This appears in just about any book about plants and gardens, as well as on seed packages, in catalogs, and on the Web. The USDA revises the map every fifteen years or so; the latest version is dated 1990 with a new one in progress but not released as of this writing.

The map divides the United States and Canada into eleven zones based on average lowest temperature, with Zone One being the arctic and Zone Eleven being frost-free. In 2006 the National Arbor Day Foundation used the same data as USDA to create an updated zone map as well as one that illustrates the differences that have developed over the past fifteen years. Meanwhile, the American Horticultural Society has put out a Heat-Zone Map to round out the picture.

Out West, where dramatic topography creates microclimates galore, gardeners depend on the *Western Garden Book* compiled by the editors of *Sunset* magazine (see Resources). This tome defines zones more precisely than the national maps, and includes an encyclopedia, separate guides to plant selection and gardening techniques, a glossary, and information about public and historic gardens. If an equivalent guide to eastern, northern, or southern gardens exists, I haven't found it yet.

I sure could have used such a guide when I moved to Vermont! While microclimates aren't as extreme here as they are out West, they nonetheless define my world. The 1990 USDA map puts our location in Zone Four (coldest range: minus twenty to minus thirty degrees Fahrenheit), which matches our weather, albeit rarely. Same is true for the frost-date maps derived from the same data. Then why, I wondered, do all the Zone Four perennials I put in fail to survive or thrive?

Eventually I inventoried the robust species already in place and discovered that all are rated for Zone Three (minus thirty to minus forty degrees Fahrenheit). Thereafter, I limited myself to Zone Three plants for anything new—and they are doing fine. Meanwhile, the 2006 Arbor Day map shows the area to be even milder. Hah! Tell that to my backyard!

Still, the zonal bands work on a gross scale and serve as a guideline. Understanding the subtleties between zones comes from experience and frame of reference.

I hail from Zone Five in central Connecticut. During my childhood we marked the passage of time with the usual rituals, such as holidays and birthdays. Four of the five birthdays in my family fell within February and March, and we correlated seasonal developments with those dates. The first robin always arrived, or the first crocus always emerged, by my mother's birthday in late February. Whichever of the two didn't happen at that time always occurred by my birthday, three weeks later.

Decade after decade these events took place by the designated times. I moved to other areas of Connecticut, then spent ten years in the Hudson Valley area of New York State, yet the robins and crocuses always arrived as they had before. I came to rely on them with the confidence I feel for sunrise and sunset. So when I moved to Vermont, I expected the same pattern.

After all, the distance from home was approximately the same as where I'd lived in New York—only one hundred and fifty road miles, substantially fewer as the crow files—and the region's terrain and climate are similar. Ditto for native flora and fauna. I knew that Vermont's more northerly position made for longer and colder winters, shorter and cooler summers. Knowing that, however, did not prepare me for what it really means.

The robins arrive two to four weeks later than in Connecticut. Crocuses don't even grow in my yard. Frost comes as late as

Memorial Day weekend, and has been recorded in June. Foliage starts turning in August.

This shouldn't have surprised me. But it did, because I formulated my expectations from the wrong map. I used the U.S. geographical map, not the zone map. When you compare the little bitty New England states tucked up there in the corner to the gigantic states in the Midwest and West (and, to a lesser degree, in the South), the distances in the Northeast are nothing! We can drive from the coast to the Canadian border inside a day. Then, when you compare our region to the scope of the world, we're a dot. From this perspective, it seemed logical to me that our cluster of states would share the same weather. But what I failed to consider was contour of the land.

The southern New England and New York of my experience are hilly—rolling hills, with many watercourses and much farmland. In Vermont, the hills are high enough that people call them mountains. Rivers must carve their way through, with little room for floodplains. The only softly rounded, open land is near the "sixth great lake," Lake Champlain.

Areas that look just like my home turf lie several hundred feet higher in altitude as well as one or more degrees of latitude farther north. And the steep ups and downs create crevices that fall into shadow early and hold their chill longer. Continuously changing topography accelerates winds and shifts their direction.

Result? A short growing season, lots of shade, and endless microclimates.

Which cycles me back around to the inescapable fact of gardens: Your experience will always be unique. No matter which route you take into a garden, you will never stop learning and will always be surprised. And you'll never run out of conversation fodder with other gardeners, for their experience can only parallel yours, never duplicate it.

By opening your heart to the living green world, you will get back twice what you put into it, and at least half of that not what you expect. Your private exchange will enable you to transfer lessons learned into life's other arenas. Gardens can teach you, feed you, comfort you, challenge you, and heal you.

What other pastime offers that?

*   ❀   *

There is something about puttering in the dirt that's therapeutic. Gloves are good, but the dirt really needs to get under the fingernails if I am to get the full benefit. I don't mean to say that there is some beneficial ingredient in the soil that can be absorbed through one's skin (although there are those who make this claim). I mean the feel of the dirt when it's cool and damp conjures up warm fuzzies that hearken back to childhood—to a time when I would putter in the dirt while my father tended his roses or harvested asparagus with his pocketknife.

It doesn't even need to be my dirt, so long as I have permission to putter in it. So my present arrangement suits me just fine. I have no garden of my own, but I help my friend Stella with hers. She is ninety-seven years old and happy to have some help, not fussy about what we grow and tolerant of my leaving the seed pods on a while, if they are decorative. I suppose this plan wouldn't do at all for some gardeners, but all I need is an occasional excuse to pick, clip, and do a little pulling or harassing of weeds.

I love the surprise of turning the corner and seeing that the scabiosa is about to blossom. "Just how did that happen while my back was turned?" I don't know exactly what it is that cheers my soul, but it has something to do with an earlier generation. And I am comforted knowing that the next generation also feels the same healing pleasure.

Jean McKinney / Portland, Oregon

NINE

Lunch on the Lawn

Advice on dandelions:
if you can't beat them, eat them.
—DR. JAMES DUKE

Thousands of years ago, our ancestors foraged for or cultivated their foods and medicines, or else they died.

Here in the twenty-first century, in the industrialized world,
most of us are so far up the food chain we have no clue where
our meals come from, or how the raw ingredients are made. Or
even how they're packaged and delivered.

What used to be a constant, cumulative education built into
everyday life is now a specialty field one must go out of one's
way to enter—to the point where the majority of us would starve
to death surrounded by bounty if we were dropped into the
wilderness and left to fend for ourselves.

God placed mankind in the Garden of Eden. Whether you are
skeptical, as many people are today, or a believer, as I am, that
garden is embedded in the human consciousness. And, since

being cast out of that garden (either literally or figuratively, as you prefer), humanity has been urgently seeking a way back in. From the Hanging Gardens of Babylon to a potted tomato plant on a high-rise balcony, almost every person has had some connection to a garden.

I mostly look at gardens with an archaeologist's eye, having been in that profession for more than a dozen years and avocationally involved for most of my life. Not only stone tools and ancient stone structures concern today's archaeologist. Pollen samples and minute plant fragments are of even greater interest. Wherever excavation is conducted in the world today, the early horticultural endeavors of prehistoric people are a high priority. Evidence increases annually showing how sitting down to dinner this evening is possible only because people thousands of years in the past began gardening instead of relying on the "nuts and berries" provided sparingly by nature.

The garden at our place is a work in progress. On a little more than ten acres, we have a variety of garden styles. The greater part is "contrived nature," similar in concept to those perfect man-made wild places found most notably in Japan. Our glacial erratic boulders are not exactly where the glacier dropped them and trees not normally neighbors grow in a "natural" forest. In the meadow, medicinal herbs discovered by Native Americans grow harmoniously in proximity to those used by my European ancestors thousands of years ago. The narrow game-trail that winds through it all was only partly made by the hooves of deer, and the poison ivy still flourishes there but has been convinced to part in places to let us pass.

Then there is what most folks would say is our garden. Not counting the lilac beds surrounding the house and flower-borders around the yard, we have a forty-by-forty fenced and cultivated space in the backyard. My wife and I split this fifty-fifty. She was taught by her father, who fed a large family significantly from the family garden, how to arrange the row crops, hill the squash and potatoes, and keep the weeds out. She works long hours tending her half and we get a great reward for her efforts. My half was intended to be along the lines of a Shaker-style herb garden. The herbs are there—the fennel and the coneflowers stand out most, the camomile, borage, oregano, and lemon balm are doing OK lower down, and there's a half-dozen others not doing quite so well. Just that I've been a little too busy to work in there lately, so at the moment my half is more a useful collection of plants resembling a field than an actual garden.

Our garden, however, all of it, is a reflection of mankind's effort to get back to that original Garden. We have little bits of our collective history represented wherever we go here. Food, medicine, and those more ethereal qualities that people have sought from gardens throughout our history are all represented, and rarely do I walk through it without being so reminded!

Dave Kieber / Darien Center, New York

Common Edibles and Medicinals

A survival skills instructor I know said, "The more you carry in your head, the less you have to carry on your back." This truth is based on the understanding that Earth itself is the grandest garden of all, which feeds all who dwell upon it. Yet we don't have to venture into the wilderness to feed ourselves directly, nor take up agriculture. Enough food to sustain a family grows right outside the average person's door.

Take the *dandelion*, a ubiquitous weed considered by many a scourge to be eradicated from lawns. Me, I look at dandelions and see free food.

Dandelions purportedly were brought to the United States as a food for honeybees. Now they are found in every state and, in fact, all over the world. You can eat them, drink them, and use them for medicine. Parts of the plant are edible all year: leaves in the spring (raw in salads or cooked like spinach), buds and flowers in the early summer (boiled, pickled, or batter-dipped and fried), roots throughout the cold season (roasted and ground into a coffee substitute).

Medicinally, dandelions are honored for their cleansing properties. The leaves are used as a diuretic—adding potassium to the body, in contrast to other diuretics that leach potassium. This quality of drawing out bad stuff while putting in good stuff makes the dandelion helpful in treating high blood pressure, detoxifying liver and kidneys and gall bladder, easing constipation, and generally reducing fluids that cause inflammation and pain, such as arthritis and gout.

So if you absolutely *must* have a green carpet for a front yard, set aside a corner to let the dandelions grow. Heck, give them pride of place and show them off to your neighbors, start a trend! The day may come when you need something dandelions have to offer.

Another plant that most of us walk over, mow down, or dig out is the *plantain*. You might already partake of it (or one of its relatives) unaware, for its seed husks form the basis of bulk laxatives. As well, plantain's young leaves can be eaten raw in a salad or boiled like spinach, as with dandelions. But plantain is better known for its healing properties: grab a leaf, squish it until juicy, and plop it on a wound for instant poultice. It also draws the venom from stings and bites, dries out poison ivy blisters, and heals fungal conditions.

Jewelweed (a.k.a. touch-me-not) works the same way: grab, squish, and apply—famous as an antidote for poison ivy rash and nettle stings, but can be used for most skin irritations. It too can be eaten as a cooked green.

Down in swamps, along riversides and pond fringes, you'll find the supermarket of wild foods, *cattails*. These plants offer something edible any time of the year. Young shoots and stalks in the springtime can be peeled to eat raw or cook like asparagus. Moving into summer, the green flower spikes, still in their sheaths, can be cooked and eaten like corn on the cob. Once the flower spikes have emerged, the pollen can be gathered, dried, and used as flour. In fall, edibility moves to the roots. A little sprout known as the horn forms on the tip of the rootstock. These sprouts, which last all winter, can be eaten raw or boiled like any tuber. The main rootstock gains starch over the winter that can be dried into flour. Then the cycle starts all over again.

Another year-round food source is the *white pine*. It can be distinguished from other evergreens by its long needles, five to a cluster. They can be made into a tea loaded with vitamins, especially vitamin C—twenty-five times that of an orange of the equivalent amount—while the inner bark can be made into flour (and a cough syrup). Young male pinecones—the small, pollen-producing catkins, not the woody female cones that bear seeds—can be boiled in an emergency. All pines are edible in similar ways.

Most of the evergreen trees offer food and/or medicine. The *balsam fir*, our most common Christmas tree, whose boughs adorn the holidays, provides unpalatable but nourishing survival food in its bark and sap. One teaspoon of the sap provides all the vitamins and minerals the human body needs for a day! And if you pop and drain the blisters found on the outer bark during summer, you've got an instant liquid bandage. Year-round you can get an astringent for wound treatment by scraping bark off the *eastern hemlock* (which also provides a nutritious tea and edible inner bark).

Nut trees, of course, drop their acorns and butternuts and beechnuts, etc., for easy pickings during autumn. Depending on the species, nuts can be roasted and eaten, or boiled and ground into flour. Walnuts are palatable raw, if you can get them open! Many of the nut trees, such as the hickory, produce edible sap during springtime. Notably, sycamore sap gives pure water for drinking and cooking. Nut kernels from the beech can be squeezed into a vegetable oil for cooking.

The more familiar *maples* and *birches* all produce edible sap and potable water.

Spring and summer are the food bonanza in the wild just as in domestic gardens. For best selection, look near water and anywhere humans have disturbed the ground. Want a salad? Mix up some *greens*—from sheep sorrel, winter cress, chicory, common evening primrose, peppergrass, oxeye daisy, wild lettuce, dandelion, burdock, thistle, toothwort—with *roots* from Queen Anne's lace (the wild carrot), Indian cucumber, wild onion and leek, evening primrose, and, surprisingly, burdock. Many of these cook up the same way as garden vegetables: steamed, boiled, stir-fried. You can also eat flowers: frittered daylily, milkweed, and dandelion; candied violets.

The aromatic *milkweed* provides food and medicine in all its components. Besides the edible flowers just mentioned, milkweed's young leaves, shoots, and pods all can be eaten. In fact, common milkweed has been called "poor man's asparagus," referring to the shoots when they're very young and the tender leaves are curled close to the stem. The immature pods make a side dish that tastes somewhat like okra.

Milkweed is named for the sticky white juice in its stems and leaves, a lightly toxic, bitter latex neutralized by boiling. During rubber shortages in World War II, this latex was trialed as a rubber substitute; in the same period, milkweed floss was used in life vests and other gear for U.S. troops, substituting for kapok. It has been shown to be better a better insulator than down.

The latex can serve as a natural bandage for wounds owing to its quick-drying elasticity that doesn't wash off. It serves the plant by deterring insects and grazing animals with its bitter taste. Only Monarch butterflies can eat it; in turn, they become bad-tasting and toxic themselves, protecting them against predators. It is believed that the Monarch's bright colors, in both butterfly and caterpillar form, send a signal that they are not good to eat.

Medicinally, milkweed can be used topically to treat warts, moles, and ringworm, and internally has been used by Native Americans as a laxative and diuretic; by early American physicians for asthma and rheumatism, as well as for other maladies.

Another common field plant, the *mullein*, is a living pharmacopoeia. These columnar plants, which can reach to eight feet tall, grow in poor soils and yet give health from their rootstock to their crowning spike. Mashed raw leaves: pain reliever for earache and toothache, poultice, and antiseptic bandage. Whole raw leaves: shoe liner (fatigue relief and insulation), wrap for sprains, fractures, and wounds. Dried leaves and flowers: teas for sore throat, congestion, asthma, coughs, diarrhea, kidney infections, and just a plain relaxing drink. Raw flowers: wart removal. Mature root: blood purifier. Dried seed spike: dip in grease to make a torch, while dried leaves can be rolled into wicks.

Many, many plants can be used to make teas, even if their other parts are inedible. If the teas aren't medicinal, they're probably loaded with vitamins or something good for you, such as with the brambles, the mints, and the pines. Sarsaparilla, meanwhile, can be made into a root beer, whereas sumac, when its fuzzy maroon heads are just right, can be soaked then strained into "Indian lemonade." Dandelion and chicory roots can be roasted then ground into coffee substitutes. Thistle stems, before the plant flowers, are packed with water.

All these plants can be found throughout the temperate United States. The more extreme environments in the country's corners—the steamy deep South, the arid desert West, the frigid arctic North—plus the alpine and coastal regions, require plants to specialize and limit their range. Get a field guide covering your own quadrant before you go looking. And don't start eating *anything* until you've learned positive ID.

The standard starting point is the Peterson's field guide series: *Wildflowers, Edible Wild Plants,* and *Medicinal Plants* (see Resources). The "Edible" book is particularly helpful, in that it includes sections on where different plants tend to grow and in what seasons which parts can be eaten.

When I lived in upstate New York, about a third of the way between Utica and the end of the earth, my wife and I had an herb business. Our gardens were both extensive and intensive, with production beds for annual culinary herbs, annual everlastings, and perennials for drying. But we also had a teaching garden, where we had specimens of hundreds of varieties of herbs in all categories, from common mints and thymes to the most obscure medicinals.

We took school groups and garden clubs and random visitors through the teaching garden and explained about the various kinds of plants. With the smallest children, it was enough to have them scratch and sniff an assortment of leaves and wonder at the intense fragrances. With older groups, we could educate them a bit about the economic plants—the dyer's and weaver's herbs, the medicinals, the perfumer's and brewer's and distiller's herbs, and so forth. With these, it was obvious that we humans selected them for cultivation because of their practical value.

But why did we settle on the beverage and culinary herbs, the ones we use now only to brew a tisane or to add a little piquancy or a subtle sweetness to a dish of meat or vegetables? This question always drew blank stares. "They taste good" was the usual

Edible Flowers

response. Yes, of course. But why did we decide that these tastes are pleasant? What was the evolutionary process that led us to that conclusion? The surprising answer is that virtually all of what we now think of as culinary herbs began, in fact, as medicinal herbs. We learned to cultivate them because they helped to ward off or cure diseases, and only as our general diet improved and we moved into the era of scientific medicine—quite recently in human history—did we relegate these old standbys to their modern culinary role.

The small number of herbs we now call medicinals are the subset that don't taste good. Two hundred years ago, they were not grown separately from thyme or parsley or mint.

Our little teaching garden was a community resource. Many a graduate of the local high school stopped by to thank us over the years and recalled some fact from the tour they took as a first-grader.

Dick Margulis / New Haven, Connecticut

Fruits

The transition from buying fruit at the supermarket to picking it in the wild is easy and direct. Blueberries—strawberries—raspberries—apples look the same in either place, unlike wild lettuce, which bears little resemblance to the bowling-ball-sized heads found in the store! And many people still venture out in the summer to gather fruit from a patch in the back forty or a pick-your-own farm down the road.

For the most part, wild berries are smaller than cultivated varieties. (Though there are exceptions; from some fluke combination of conditions this year, we got a patch of red raspberries that produced the largest berries I've ever seen, a full inch long!)

The brambles form a huge class of edible plants. They comprise three broad groups—raspberries, blackberries, and dewberries—all arching shrubs distinguished mainly by their stems and fruits. There's also a variant called purple flowering raspberry, with huge leaves like wild grape and a beautiful single flower like a rose. This plant's berries are also edible but not as tasty as those of its sisters.

I tell the base groups apart by their fundamentals. Raspberries have round stems and almost no prickers; you can wade through a thicket without getting scratched, while blackberries are larger, more aggressive bushes with thick, angular stems bearing nasty thorns. Dewberries are creepers.

Raspberries have a milky white glaze on their stems that's actually a yeast, useful in survival scenarios. Their leaves make a tea that is good for treating diarrhea and "female complaints." The fruit forms a hollow center when separated from the stalk. Blackberries lack the waxy glaze and hollow center but otherwise include the same edible and medicinal properties. (Interesting trivia: North American blackberries produce an edible purple dye used by the USDA for labeling meats.)

The other common aggregate fruit, wild strawberry, is a ground-trailer instead of a bush but for the rest is consumed like the raspberries and blackberries: eaten fresh, made into jams and jellies, and the leaves used for tea. An extract of the wild straw-berry leaf is exceptionally high in vitamin C, which infuses into the tea. Unlike most other fruits, the wild strawberry leaf is avail-able under snow and can be gathered year-round.

Blueberries, too, make a valuable tea, good for diabetics because it helps regulate sugar. The berries, of course, are tasty as-is or baked into pies, muffins, and cobblers, or cooked into jams. These single, blue, berries come in many varieties—high bush, low bush, huckleberries, bilberries, deerberries. All are considered nutrition powerhouses.

Likewise cranberries, those tart red berries found in boggy places, best known for their medicinal use as a treatment for uri-nary tract infections, and for their edible use as a condiment in holiday meals. Unlike with blueberries, the highbush variety is unrelated—a viburnum—named "highbush cranberry" because of the similarly red, tart berries, which can be substituted for the original in all applications: juice, jelly, sauce.

Other, lesser known berries abound in the wild—gooseberry, nannyberry, partridgeberry, currant, serviceberry, Juneberry, bearberry—but these are best approached with a really good guidebook or teacher, or else ignored. Once outside the familiar equivalents to supermarket fruits, you enter the Russian roulette game of look-alikes.

Consider grapes, elderberries, and cherries. Two of these are familiar to most everyone, especially the grape. All wild grapes are edible, and during food-scarce winter, their dehydrated fruits make a serviceable tea. However, Canada moonseed looks a lot like wild grape at first glance. If you don't know that grapes twine with tendrils and moonseed twines with its stem, you could be in for a bellyache—or a trip to the hospital, depending on how much you eat.

Wild cherries, like all stone fruits (cherries, apples, apricots, peaches, plums, pears), contain low levels of hydrogen cyanide in their bark and pits. The human digestion system is equipped to deal with this in small doses. But watch it with the leaves and bark. Few people even attempt to eat these parts of a cherry; however, livestock can get into it and die. The undamaged leaves of wild black cherry contain a cyanide precursor that turns toxic when the leaves are damaged. Cyanide is present, too, in elderberry leaves, twigs, and seeds, demanding great care when one makes elderberry wine or jelly. As well, there are two kinds of elderberry, red and common. Common has purple-black berries that are safe when ripe, whereas the red is poisonous. Thus, edible wild foods must be approached with knowledge and respect (see Rules of Thumb, below).

The stone fruits mentioned above, aside from cherries, plums, and crab apples, aren't commonly found in the wild, save as remnants of abandoned orchards or escapes spread by seed. Here in New England, domestic apples survive in the midst of second- and third-growth forest along with the stone walls that once marked boundaries of pioneer farms. Their fruit now feeds wildlife or the occasional resourceful person willing to make applesauce or apple butter.

In Phoenix, Arizona, some people claim that oranges grow wild. But they, too, are leftovers from another time. Phoenix arose not from ashes, like the phoenix of legend, but from desert, becoming an oasis thanks to the Salt River. Its water supported the plants indigenous to the desert—organ-pipe cactus, sage, and their ilk—but its seasonal flux couldn't support what farmers wanted to grow. So Roosevelt Dam was built to harness the river, part of a massive project including canals to channel the waters for irrigation. Thus, vast desert acreage bloomed into groves of grapefruit, oranges, and cotton.

The contrasts of lush agriculture framed by stark, muted colors of desert and mountains created a beauty that drew more people. And more people . . . carving the fields and groves into housing developments, roads, and sewers. Now all that remains of the citrus glory are random trees found in schoolyards and parks—Phoenix's "wild" oranges.

Rules of Thumb

First rule: It is *not* safe to randomly experiment. Understand what you're doing before you play with wild foods; and understand that acquiring this knowledge takes time. Within that proscription, you can work with certain universals. For example, if it looks and smells like onion or garlic, it's edible. All mints have a square stem and can be used for teas, several of which have medicinal properties. And while humans can't eat grass, lacking the stomach structure to digest the cellulose, we can eat all grass seeds (generally as flour). All mustards have edible components. Ditto pines.

To learn something about plants as families, and thereby many general facts about their properties, consult the wonderful *Botany in a Day: The Patterns Method of Plant Identification*. As its author, Thomas J. Elpel, states: "One principle I have learned while writing and teaching is that the ease or difficulty of learning a subject is not so much a factor of the complexity or volume of the information, but rather of its packaging."

Elpel thus composed a reference volume that organizes plants by their shared attributes, enabling the student to learn more in one gulp than by years of identifying one species at a time. Learning the seven key patterns opens the door to recognizing forty-five thousand species! This book also gives an overview of plant evolution and the relationship between the plant and animal kingdoms, while explaining how the scientific classification system works. It functions as both a field guide and a condensed educational text.

Foragers must understand that domestic varieties of wild plants may not contain the same elements as their cousins. Garden plants have been cultivated to enhance specific features, such as blossom and fruit size or disease resistance, at the cost of another feature. Note also that plants will suck up toxins that pass through their environments. Therefore, avoid eating anything from along roadsides, or from lawns or fields that have been treated with pesticides. Be careful, too, around swampy areas, where polluted runoffs often accumulate.

Other caveats for foraging: Not all berries are edible and many are toxic. Avoid any white berries, period. Conversely, all aggregate fruits are edible. Look up the rest before experimenting. And don't eat any mushrooms! You need specialized knowledge in order to pick and prepare fungi safely. All food foraging requires knowledge, but mushrooms in particular demand expertise. Mistakes can be fatal.

The reason that using plants for food and medicine takes a lifetime to master is because so many of them look alike and their useful parts can shift with the seasons. Something tasty in the spring can be poisonous in the fall!

For the most part, though, the plant kingdom offers a benign banquet. Some wild foods are prized by gourmets and offered in the finest restaurants. Each spring I see the fiddleheads of ostrich fern in the grocery store. For the rest, you have to go get them, which is easier than it sounds, for a wild smorgasbord lies within a mile of most anyone's house.

TEN

Why Bother?

Man—despite his artistic pretensions, his sophistication,
and his many accomplishments—owes his existence
to a six-inch layer of topsoil and the fact it rains.

—UNKNOWN

Scientists estimate that three hundred sixty-five thousand species of wild plant grow in the world—probably more, since some remain unidentified. Of these, approximately two-thirds are considered edible. (Edible does not mean "tasty," by the way. Only that you can consume it without harm.) That's a lot of free food! But you need to study if you want to start foraging. The education is worth it, though, because knowing how to take care of yourself is empowering.

Therein lies the value of opening your heart to gardens. Empowerment can be gained through involvement with plants, and feeling empowered does more for your mental and physical health than anything else.

It's particularly important these days, when we often feel overwhelmed by life and frightened by our dependency on invisible people and institutions. One shudders at the thought of, for example, what might happen if the power grid went down for a few weeks, especially in the city. Bad enough when it happens for just a few days!

Reflecting back on recent disasters . . . hurricanes, floods, tornadoes, wildfires . . . ice storms and blizzards . . . bombings, riots, strikes . . . big troubles hover dangerously close on any given day, any of which can take out our infrastructure of goods and services. How many of us know how to survive without them? Or what if an accident isolated us from help for days?

Knowing even a few common plants to eat or treat a wound with can get you through a horrendous experience. This applies over the longer term, as well, when you consider global warming. The Arbor Day Zone Map, mentioned in chapter eight, shows an across-the-board rise in temperatures over the past decade. During this period, many gardeners, along with birdwatchers and ecologists of all stripes, have observed species extending (or contracting) their ranges because of climate change. With it comes new insect pests, dramatic shifts in precipitation patterns, and crop failures, all of which can upheave agriculture and economy. Nobody will be unaffected over time.

I get depressed and jittery any time I think of such things. But fear is the path to empowerment, and you can get there through plants.

Just as pain is the body's way of signaling that something's wrong, fear is the psyche's cue to act. As individuals, there's not much we can do to save the world. However, each of us can take care of our own little corner of it, and let our overlapping circles of influence build positive momentum.

But how?

By engaging with plants. As discussed in chapter seven, it's all about your nature. Your resources. Your passions. Acting, then, can be as simple as allowing dandelions into your lawn or as radical as devoting your life to sustainable development. If you don't want to or can't garden, plant a tree in someone's memory, or support others' more complex efforts by contributing time or money. Sometimes it's enough to just applaud loudly and pass the word. Perhaps help remove obstacles in other people's way.

One thing anyone can do is learn a few wild edibles (cultivate them, too, in corners of our private territory or by encouraging others to let wild plants to thrive in larger unused lands, thereby preserving an alternative food supply). Investing some time to know what grows in these corners, and what parts of the plants can be used during what seasons, could pay you back some day. In the meantime, you can enjoy a hobby that will keep you learning for the rest of your life. Between identifying and gathering and processing, wild foods involve art and craft and science and all your senses. It's a great activity to do with kids, a legacy more enduring than anything material you can give.

Hobby-level gardeners can focus on building and maintaining healthy soil, which sustains healthy plants, which in turn resist insect and weather extremes. We can grow food and learn how to preserve it so there will always be something in the larder, and grow more than we need so to share with others, either as a gift or as revenue to support our households. We can cultivate native flowers, shrubs, and trees, because they are more resilient than exotics and afford food and shelter for wildlife. Throughout, we can train ourselves to think always in terms of water: how to capture it, distribute it without waste, keep it clean, keep it in the ground rather than letting it wash away nutrients (and our houses).

An experiment involving runoff from a Connecticut suburb into Long Island Sound shows the value of gardens in this context. State agencies undertook a ten-year study of two subdivisions, one constructed with the conventional sealed-pavement road and driveways, curbs and storm drains; the other clustered so that road and driveways were shared, made of crushed stone or pavers instead of asphalt, surrounded by smaller lawns with some wild areas set aside. In addition, curbs were replaced with grassy swales to slow and absorb surface runoff, matched by a "rain garden" for each property that collected runoff from house and lot.

Runoff carries bacteria and chemicals such as fertilizers, automotive fluids, and road salt into the watershed, harming water quality and aquatic life, ultimately our own lives. No sweeping solution has yet been found, but like so many big problems it can be pecked away at by individuals and institutions. In this case, the alternative-style development proved itself by holding runoff to the same levels that existed *before* construction, whereas the conventional setup contributed more runoff—exacerbating the problem instead of helping solve it. The experiment demonstrates how greenery protects us as well as feeds us and adds beauty. Plants are the Earth's lungs and water filters, no way around that fact.

You can manage runoff yourself by adding a rain garden to a low spot in your yard and installing native plants. (See Resources for links to technical information.) Options exist for larger-scale wastewater management—witness Anna Edey, who describes in her book, *Solviva: How to Grow $500,000 on One Acre and Peace on Earth*, how she conceived and executed virtually waste-free, non-polluting water systems for household plumbing and plant irrigation. Not only that, she designed equivalent systems for rural, suburban, and urban environments around the world, which "can save thousands for a family, millions for a community, billions for a nation, as well as prevent the use of toxic chemicals . . . In addition, important fertilizer resources and water are saved and made available for beautifying the landscapes."

One woman's vision and labor can have that much impact. That is, if we listen and learn.

Another lone woman—celebrity singer and actor Bette Midler—cleaned up portions of New York City. She created the New York Restoration Project in response to her dismay upon moving there and seeing so much garbage and waste. Her "Conservancy of Forgotten Places" now reclaims city parks and open spaces that have fallen into disuse owing to lack of funds and public interest. The organization also has revitalized community gardens around the city, enabling "oases of vegetables, fruits, flowers and tranquility in neighborhoods where concrete otherwise rules."

On the industrial side, groups of scientists have generated another ray of hope. Ever heard of phytoremediation? It's a term so new it's not yet in the dictionary. It means using plants to clean up the environment. In their never-ending process of drawing water and chemicals from the soil, storing and converting them, and passing them into the air, plants not only can capture contaminants, as in the rain gardens, but also extract them from air, soil, and water, cleaning and restoring the environment. So far, more than four hundred plants have been identified and/or harnessed toward this end.

The same idea applies in recovery farming. Plants can, for example, withdraw trace gold from exhausted mines, simultaneously restoring the land and providing revenue to pay for it and jobs for the impoverished people left behind when the mine closed. The process, called phytomining, has real commercial potential, especially in fueling the growing demands of nanotechnology. So far, oats have proven the best at sucking up gold.

Brake fern, another "hyperaccumulator," works with arsenic, cleaning up fifty times its weight worth of soil. Sunflowers have been employed in cleaning radioactive elements out of ponds, and, in conjunction with mustard plants, have cleaned up accumulations of lead. Poplar trees, capable of pumping twenty-five gallons of water daily through their deep roots, pull out trichloroethylene (a dry-cleaning chemical). Pennycress works for zinc, cadmium, and nickel.

Knowing all this makes it hard to ignore plants and easy to honor them. It's easy, also, to invite them into our lives. Once we've struck up a relationship with them, we center ourselves on the planet a bit better, gaining the confidence and optimism needed to pass successfully through life. Opening your heart to plants helps open your mind; open your eyes; open your energy channels, all of which allow good things to happen. And good things tend to beget more good things, leading to the health and happiness we all crave.

I have always had a great love and appreciation of plants. This is because I find them to be very nourishing. Yes, I grow a vegetable garden every year and it provides me with a most nourishing harvest. But I don't mean that kind of nourishing. Plants nourish my soul.

I remember playing in the neighbor's hayloft as a child; the smell of a newly mowed hayfield brings back pleasant memories of that time. I would also spend all day picking wild strawberries, all the while anticipating the strawberry shortcake I'd be having for dessert that night with homemade biscuits and freshly whipped cream. I'd gaze in awe at a bird's nest tucked away up in a tree. It was constructed of various plant material and I was amazed at how carefully it was woven together and stayed in place so well. Most of my childhood memories include plants!

I've had a garden now for many years and I find it very relaxing to be out there digging in the dirt. If I'm having a bad day, it's soon forgotten when I'm gardening. I watch the insects that live among my veggies; their lives intertwined with the plants. I have a small garter snake living in a "toad abode," a small clay house more decorative than functional. But it seems someone's using it, and I'm thrilled to see him every now and then.

Being out there just makes me feel good. It's also very rewarding when I eat a fresh salad utilizing veggies that I've just picked. I always plant several rows of sunflowers too, so the birds will have something to look forward to when the seeds ripen. I don't want to be the only one enjoying the fruits of my labor.

I'm fortunate to have many wild plants around me. Pretty soon I'll be trekking out to a favorite spot to pick highbush cranberries. These I'll freeze until Thanksgiving where they'll be a welcome addition to my Thanksgiving feast. Next spring I'll await the first dandelions; the young leaves lend a fresh taste to any salad.

I could never imagine my life without plants. I eat them, I smell them, I grow them, I love looking at them. Plants are very important to us; we couldn't live without them. To answer your questions: "What do you do with plants?" I enjoy them. "Why?" Because they nourish my soul.

Aggie Simon / Wilderness Learning Center,
Chateaugay, New York

Epilogue

Of all the wonderful things in the wonderful universe of God,
nothing seems to me more surprising than the planting
of a seed in the blank earth and the result thereof.

—JULIE MOIR MESSERVY

My heart opened to gardens when I wasn't looking. The process started early in my life, with a general sense of well-being when I was outdoors. As I grew, the feeling began to focus into sensory delight: The happy crunch of leaves underfoot, and their bedazzling fall colors; the brilliant blue of a cloudless sky, and the eerily beautiful, deep indigo of full-moon shadows thrown across snow; the pale, pale tinge of pink inside a white peony, and the surprise scent of rose when you touch your nose to it and inhale; the hundred shades of green, so vivid they threaten to burst, as spring gains hold on the land and everything is growing as vigorously as it can.

Eventually curiosity wakened. What's that? I kept wondering, then looked it up if no one could tell me. After I knew one plant's name, I wanted to know them all. Soon I wanted to know why that plant grew here but not there, or whether you could eat it.

That led to favorites, which, I learned upon attaining adulthood, I could actually cause to grow in my personal space! No longer did I have to wait to chance upon them.

During the many years that passed before I owned personal growing space, I grabbed it where I could. Sometimes this amounted to nurturing a single jade plant or aloe plant in a dusty window. Other times I secretly buried bulbs around the base of an apartment building where gardens were forbidden. Once my apartment came with a whole strip of grass along a sidewalk, which I ripped out and replaced with a little flower and vegetable garden, only to have the blossoms and fruits get snipped off by passing college students. Always, no matter where I lived, there was God's Garden, and Other People's Gardens, to be viewed and inhaled and enjoyed.

Finally, I had my own garden—actually, half a dozen plots spread around several acres—and embarked upon the adventures of discovery recounted in this book. Yet I never considered myself a gardener, because working with plants wasn't my consuming passion. I believed you had to feel that passion in order to qualify as a gardener, especially to be dubbed "a green thumb."

Many more years passed before I realized that passion doesn't have to burn inside like a forest fire; rather, it can smolder quietly, like an internal, warming ember. And that's how it was with me. Every time I thought about not doing a garden this year, my heart rebelled. I *had* to have flowers in the spring. I *had* to have vegetables in the summer. I *had* to tidy it all up and wave it goodbye in the fall. I *had* to plan the next one during the winter. I didn't burn to spend all my free time doing it, but I had to do it somehow, in some way.

This came as a surprise. Why was having a garden so important? Because that's how I measure time, and how I stay connected to my humanity—that is, my humanness, a child of the universe in self-aware mammal form. I am cousin to the plants and animals and birds and bugs despite physical isolation from them brought by all the miracles of today's world that keep us warm and safe and dry and fed. Yet the natural cycles of day to night, spring-summer-fall-winter, birth-growth-death-rebirth, run constant through our lives no matter what else is going on. So keeping a garden keeps me in tune.

Understanding moved me to intent. Now I make sure that I garden, whether I'm in the mood or not. A measure of its healing force is the number of times I start out not-in-the-mood and end up not wanting to stop! On some days, my mind goes blissfully blank and I become a simple, sensate organism; on other days, the physical work channels thoughts into new directions, so that I emerge from a session with fresh ideas to solve old problems, or inspiration to follow into all-new directions.

Throughout, the curiosity that got me started continues unabated. That curiosity, along with immersion in the cycles of life, keeps joy bubbling beneath my diaphragm and my vision looking ever forward. Mostly, though, this act of keeping in tune with life holds me in an active state of appreciation of life—my own, and all others'. Viewing the world from this angle opened my heart in spite of myself. I'm hoping, through this book, to share the sensation and help you find it for yourself, too.

It was so green tonight. The birds were murmuring as my little boy and I played catch out back in the twilight. Our yard was ringed with blooming iris—tall, exotic wands of peach, white, yellow, purple, blue—some solid and some bicolored. Some ruffled, all bearded, the iris added their grapey fragrance to the cool air.

But it was the smell of the neighbor's mock orange that made everything stop. That fragrance conjured up the same heavy sweetness from my childhood backyard. At that same moment, I noticed the tight-fisted pink peony bud—our first ever. It had unfurled one bright petal. Peonies, sweet smells, ruffled petals, evening, damp, green, grass, jumping boy—a riot of spring beauty.

As I was beginning to feel overcome by the glory of the moment, I realized my grandma was there. She always had something beautiful in bloom in her yard and she brought blossoms into her house throughout the green seasons. Of course she should be here. She looked at the peony first and then I helped her see every special iris, even the white one with the orange beard that was tucked behind the pear tree.

"The bridal wreath suffered in the thunderstorm," I explained, "but it was beautiful with the iris in my vase on the sideboard. The pear, apricot, and peach trees are full of young fruit. When it is really hot in August, I suppose we'll be busy canning," I continued.

I sighed and caught the ball again. Peter needed a drink, so we wandered inside. It was bedtime. I closed the screen door and looked again into the quiet, darkening yard.

"Bye, Grandma," I whispered. "Enjoy yourself. I'm so glad you came to see my garden, and my boy. We've never had this chance before. I love you. Goodnight."

Judy Reynolds / Norman, Oklahoma

A Cornucopia of Information

If you have a garden and a library,
you have everything you need.

—CICERO

There are *soooooooo* many books and magazines out there about plants, gardens, and gardening, and *soooooooo* many websites available—loaded with all the detail and viewpoints you could want—that I can't begin to list them all. You can lose yourself for days once you get started!

The World Wide Web has been likened to a humongous library with the books all scattered on the floor. Fortunately, we can find our way through that mess using search engines, such as Google. Just make your query as precise as possible—for example, typing in "gardening" brings 64,500,000 results to wade through! "Garden" brings a mere 548,000,000 results, which drops to 88,900,000 when you add an "s" to the word. Compare that to a reasonable 279 hits for "railroad gardening" (but only if you type the words inside quotation marks; leaving them off generates 1,670,000 results!).

In that context, the following combined bibliography and

"webography" seems short. I compiled it using my personal biases as a filter, aiming to include a reference on most topics touched on throughout this volume. The majority of books I can recommend from experience, whereas some were suggested by enthusiasts and others I passed while researching and thought they looked good. Some of the websites I have permanently bookmarked, and others looked like something that other people might gain value from, so I included them. Many have links to other sites supporting the subject.

All websites were confirmed "live" as of November 1, 2007. If you do hit a site that is no longer valid, keep going, for you will surely find what you're looking for somewhere else!

GENERAL GARDENING (Flowers and Vegetables)

Books

All About Ground Covers, ed. Nancy Arbuckle (Ortho Books, 1982)

Backyard Problem Solver: 2,168 Natural Solutions for Growing Great Grass, Super Shrubs, Bright Bulbs, Perfect Perennials, Amazing Annuals, Vibrant Vegetables, Terrific Trees, and Much, Much More!, Jerry Baker (American Master Products, 2002)

Cinder Block Gardens: Finally, Gardening Made Simple and Easy, The Way Gardening Should Be!, Lynn A. Gillespie (TLC Publishing, 2000)

Complete Guide to Gardening, Better Homes and Gardens (Meredith Corporation, 1979)

Container Garden Magic, Jerry Baker (Jerry Baker, 2002)

Country Wisdom Bulletin (60+ titles in Gardening category) (Storey Publishing)

Dead Snails Leave No Trails: Natural Pest Control for Home and Garden, Loren Nancarrow and Janet Hogan Taylor (Ten Speed Press, 1996)

The Encyclopedia of Planting Combinations, Tony Lord (Firefly Books, 2002)

Four-Season Harvest, Eliot Coleman (Chelsea Green, 1992)

Gardening Essentials, Barbara Pleasant (National Home Gardening Club, 2007)

Home Solar Gardening, John H. Pierce (Van Nostrand Reinhold, 1981)

Incredible Vegetables from Self-Watering Containers, Ed Smith (Storey Publishing, 2006)

Introduction to Plant Diseases: Identification and Management, 2nd ed., George B. Lucas, C. Lee Campbell, Leon T. Lucas (Van Nostrand Reinhold, 2001)

Kitchen Harvest: A Cook's Guide to Growing Organic Fruit, Vegetables and Herbs in Containers, Susan Berry (Laurel Glen Publishing, 2002; Frances Lincoln Publishers, 2007)

Landscaping with Wildflowers: An Environmental Approach to Gardening, James W. Wilson (Houghton Mifflin, 1992)

Lasagna Gardening, Patricia Lanza (Rodale, 1998)

Lasagna Gardening for Small Spaces, Patricia Lanza (Rodale, 2002)

Lasagna Gardening with Herbs, Patricia Lanza (Rodale, 2004)

New Complete Guide to Gardening, Susan A. Roth (*Better Homes and Gardens*, 1997)

Noah's Garden: Restoring the Ecology of Our Own Backyards, Sara B. Stein (Houghton Mifflin, 1995).

Rodale's Illustrated Encyclopedia of Gardening and Landscaping Techniques, Barbara W. Ellis, Ed. (MJF Books, 1990)

Secrets of Companion Planting, Louise Riotte (Garden Way, 1975) [later released as *Carrots Love Tomatoes: Secrets of Companion Planting*, Storey]

Solar Gardening: Growing Vegetables Year-Round the American Intensive Way, Leandre Poisson and Gretchen Vogel Poisson (Chelsea Green, 1994)

Solviva: How to Grow $500,000 on One Acre & Peace on Earth, Anna Edey (Trailblazer Press, 1998)

Square Foot Gardening series, Mel Bartholomew:
Square Foot Gardening (Rodale, 1981)

Cash from Square Foot Gardening (Square Foot Press, 2004)

A Teacher's Lesson Plan for Children (Square Foot Press, 1999)

All New Square Foot Gardening (Cool Springs Press, 2007)

Introduction to Square Foot Gardening, video, 2005

Square Foot Gardening, PBS Video Classic Series, 2005

Stokes Backyard Bird Book: The Complete Guide to Attracting, Identifying, and Understanding the Birds in Your Backyard, Donald and Lillian Stokes (Rodale, 2003)

Terrific Garden Tonics! 345 Do-It-Yourself, Fix 'Em Formulas for Maintaining a Lush Lawn & Gorgeous Garden, Jerry Baker (American Master Products, 2004)

The 12-Month Gardener: Simple Strategies for Extending Your Growing Season, Jeff Ashton (Lark Books, 2001)

The 20-Minute Vegetable Gardener, Tom Christopher and Marty Asher (Random House, 1999)

The Best Gardening Ideas I Know, Robert Rodale (Rodale Press, 1974)

The New Gardener, Pippa Greenwood (National Home Gardening Club, 1995)

The Natural Habitat Garden, Ken Druse (Timber Press, 2004)

The Organic Gardener's Handbook of Natural Insect and Disease Control, ed. Barbara W. Ellis and Fern Marshall Bradley (Rodale, 1996)

The Organic Lawn Care Manual, Paul Tukey (Storey Publishing, 2007)

Tips for the Lazy Gardener, Linda Tilgner (Storey Publishing, 1985)

Trowel and Error: Over 700 Tips, Remedies and Shortcuts for the Gardener, Sharon Lovejoy (Workman Publishing, 2003)

Weedless Gardening, Lee Reich (Workman Publishing, 2001)

Magazines

Better Homes and Gardens, www.bhg.com

Birds and Blooms, www.birdsandblooms.com

Country Gardens, see the Store page of the Better Homes and Gardens website, above

Fine Gardening, www.taunton.com/finegardening

Garden Design, www.gardendesign.com

Garden Gate, www.gardengatemagazine.com

Gardening How-To (magazine of the National Home Gardening Club), www.gardeningclub.com

Horticulture, www.hortmag.com

Organic Gardening, www.organicgardening.com

The Herb Quarterly, www.herbquarterly.com

Websites

American Horticultural Society: www.ahs.org

Dig in with Kym (Kym Pokorny—garden journalist): http://blog.oregonlive.com/kympokorny

Gardener's Network: www.gardenersnet.com

Gardenscape.com, Your Gardening Resource: www.gardenscape.com/GSResources.html

GardenWeb, The Internet's Garden & Home Community: www.gardenweb.com

Jerry Baker, America's Master Gardener: www.jerrybaker.com

My Garden Guide/The Daily Dirt blog: www.mygardenguide.com

National Gardening Association: www.garden.org

National Home Gardening Club: www.gardeningclub.com

Natureworks: www.naturework.com

Project Native: www.projectnative.org

Smaller American Lawns Today (S.A.L.T.): www.conncoll.edu/ccrec/greennet/arbo/salt/salt. html

Square Foot Gardening: www.squarefootgardening.com

Suite 101: Vegetable Gardens: http://vegetablegardens.suite101. com

The Garden Pest Control Center: http://garden-pest-control.biz/index.htm

USDA Cooperative State Research, Education, and Extension Service: www.csrees.usda.gov/Extension/index

U.S. Department of Agriculture Plants Database: http://plants.usda.gov

Companion Planting and Pest Control Plants:

www.ghorganics.com/page2.html

www.basic-info-4-organic-fertilizers.com/companionplants.html

www.homeandgardensite.com/companion_planting.htm

www.mail-archive.com/herb-recipe@yahoogroups.com/msg00187.html

www.pallensmith.com/index.php?option=com_content&task=view&id
=53&Itemid=96

Hanging Planters (upside-down tomatoes):

www.seedsofknowledge.com/tomato2.html

www.ehow.com/how_2062318_grow-tomatoes-upside-down-
bucket.html

http://container-gardens.suite101.com/article.cfm/turning_tomato_
growing_upside_down

www.nighthawkpublications.com/backyard/tomato.htm

Hay Bale Gardening:

www.geocities.com/teman@sbcglobal.net/haytomatoes.html

www.decaturdaily.com/decaturdaily/livingtoday/040720/bale.shtml

Lasagna Gardening:

http://ourgardengang.tripod.com/lasagna_gardening.htm

www.post-gazette.com/neigh_washington/20030921wahome5.asp

www.tbmastergardeners.homestead.com/LasagnaGardening.html

Soils and Soil Indicators:

www.demesne.info/Garden-Help/Solutions/Problem-Diagnosis.htm

www.rain.org/global-garden/weeds.html

www.readersdigest.ca/homegarden/n_homegarden_soil3.html

www.richsoil.com/lawn-care.jsp

HYDROPONICS AND WATER GARDENS

Books

Grow More Nutritious Vegetables Without Soil, James D. Taylor (Parkside Press, 1983)

Home Hydroponics . . . and How To Do It!, Lem Jones (Crown Publishers, 1977)

How-To Hydroponics, 4th ed., Keith F. Roberto (Futuregarden Press, 2003)

Hydroponic Basics: The Basics of Soilless Gardening Indoors, George F. Van Patten (Van Patten Publishing, 2004)

Hydroponic Food Production, 4th ed., Dr. Howard Resh (Woodbridge Press, 1989)

Hydroponics for the Home Gardener: An easy-to-follow, step-by-step guide for growing healthy vegetables, herbs and house plants without soil, Stewart Kenyon (Van Nostrand Reinhold, 1979; Key Porter Books, 2005)

Magazines

The Growing Edge, www.growingedge.com/magazine/index.html

Pondkeeper, www.pondkeeper.com

Ponds Magazine, www.pondsmagazine.com

Water Gardening, (no website yet)

Websites

Hydroponics:

www.ext.vt.edu/pubs/envirohort/426-084/426-084.html

http://en.wikipedia.org/wiki/Hydroponics

Water Gardens:

http://watergarden.com/pages/build_wg.html

www.lilieswatergardens.co.uk/advice.asp

www.sunterrausa.com/gardens/installation/intro.cfm

www.pondlifestyles.com

BACKYARD ORCHARDS

Books

Fruits and Berries for the Home Garden, Lewis Hill (Storey Books, 1992)

The Backyard Orchardist: A Complete Guide to Growing Fruit Trees in the Home Garden, Stella Otto (Ottographics, 1995)

The Home Orchard: Growing Your Own Deciduous Fruit and Nut Trees, C. Ingels, P. Geisel, and M. Norton (University of California Agriculture & Natural Resources, 2007)

Websites:

http://homeorchard.ucdavis.edu

www.associatedcontent.com/article/190656/your_guide_to_starting_a_ backyard_orchard.html

www.davewilson.com

www.midfex.org

EDUCATIONAL PROGRAMS

Earthwatch Institute (volunteer opportunities in the field): www.earthwatch.org/site/pp.asp?c=dsJSK6PFJnH&b=386451

Ecovolunteering: www.ecovolunteer.org

Elderhostel (specializes in educational travel for older adults): www.elderhostel.org

Environmental Schools Directory: www.enviroeducation.com

WWOOF—WorldWide Opportunities on Organic Farms: www.wwoofusa.org/what.html

HORTICULTURAL THERAPY AND THERAPEUTIC GARDENING

Accessible Gardening, Therapeutic Gardening:

www.extension.umn.edu/distribution/horticulture/DG6757.html

www.thrive.org.uk/specific-services-difficult.asp

www.carryongardening.org.uk/index.asp

www.djc.com/special/landscape98/10037844.htm

American Horticultural Therapy Association:
  www.ahta.org/information

American Occupational Therapy Foundation:
  www.aotf.org/html/gardening.shtml

Gardening for People with Impaired Vision:

www.nlb-online.org/mod.php?mod=userpage&page_id=522&menu=

www.ces.purdue.edu/vanderburgh/horticulture/garden4blind.htm

www.kab.org.uk/gardening.htm

http://lesum.de/vereine/blindengarten/index_en.htm

www.perkins.org/subsection.php?id=241 (links to gardens for the blind)

www.perkins.org/oncampus/horticulture/othergardens.html

INDOOR AND GREENHOUSE GARDENING

Books

Gardening in Your Greenhouse (Greenhouse Basics #2), Mark Freeman (Stackpole Books, 1998) [companion volume to *Building Your Own Greenhouse (Greenhouse Basics)*, Mark Freeman (Stackpole Books, 1997)]

Greenhouse Gardener's Companion: Growing Food and Flowers in Your Greenhouse or Sunspace, Shane Smith (Fulcrum Publishing, 2000)

Magazines

Greenhouse Grower, www.greenhousegrower.com

Orchids: The Magazine of the American Orchid Society,
  http://orchidweb.org/aos/publications/page01.aspx

Websites

www.evergreengardenworks.com/indoors.htm (bonsai)

www.greenhousegarden.com (greenhouses)

www.how-to-grow-orchid.com (orchids)

www.orchids.org/culture/culture.html (orchids)

www.stretcher.com/stories/960415a.cfm (micro-gardening)

www.thegardenhelper.com/terrarium.html (terrariums)

MISCELLANEOUS

Children's Memorial and Gardens: www.childrensmemorialandgarden.
  org/garden_tour.asp

Cranberry Creations: www.cranberrycreations.com

Earth Healing Institute: www.earthhealinginstitute.com

Florigraphy:

www.factmonster.com/ipka/A0767953.html

www.tickie.net/SayIt/index.html

http://tilehurst.net/infopool/flowers.html

Herbalpedia: The Ultimate Herbal Encyclopedia: www.herbalpedia.com

National Gardening Association "Adopt a School Garden" program:
  http://assoc.garden.org/ag/asg/

Natural Dyes / Art, Info, and Supplies:

http://artistsregister.com/artist_page.phtml?number=AZ104%20

www.pioneerthinking.com/naturaldyes.html

http://nyny.essortment.com/naturaldyeplan_rxll.htm

Pressing Flowers:

www.preservedgardens.com

www.flowerpressing.com/press-flowers.htm

The Daffodil Principle: www.holisticpractitionersnetwork.com/
  Articles/daffodil_principle.htm

PHYTOREMEDIATION

www.envirotools.org/factsheets/phytoremediation.shtml

www.kidsregen.org/educators/nga.php

www.aehs.com/journals/phytoremediation

PLANT IDENTIFICATION
(Garden, Wildflower, Edible, Medicinal)

Books

Botany in a Day: The Patterns Method of Plant Identification, Thomas J. Elpel (HOPS Press, 2006, 5th ed.)

Edible Wild Plants: A North American Field Guide, Thomas A. Elias and Peter A. Dykeman (Sterling Publishing Co., 1990)

Feasting Free on Wild Edibles, Bradford Angier (Stackpole Books, 1972)

Field Guide to Edible Wild Plants, Bradford Angier (Stackpole Books, 2000)

Identifying and Harvesting Edible and Medicinal Plants in Wild (and Not So Wild) Places, Steve Brill (HarperResource, 2002)

Lawn Food Cook Book (Groceries in the Backyard), Linda Runyon (Wild Foods, 1985)

Native Harvests: Recipes & Botanicals of the American Indian, E. Barrie Kavasch (Random House, 1979) [reissued as *Native Harvests: American Indian Wild Foods and Recipes* (Dover Books, 2005)]

Stalking the Wild Asparagus, Euell Gibbons (David McKay Company, 1971 ed.)

The Audubon Society Field Guide to North American Wildflowers, Eastern Region, William A. Niering and Nancy C. Olmstead (Alfred A. Knopf, 1979)

The Peterson Guides:

A Field Guide to Wildflowers/Northeastern and North-central North America, Roger Tory Peterson and Margaret McKenny (Houghton Mifflin, 1968)

A Field Guide to Edible Wild Plants/Eastern and Central North America, Lee Allen Peterson (Houghton Mifflin, 1977)

A Field Guide to Medicinal Plants/Eastern and Central North America, Steven Foster and James A. Duke (Houghton Mifflin, 1990)

Nature Study Guild Pocket Guides:

Berry Finder: A Guide to Native Plants with Fleshy Fruits, Dorcas S. Miller

Winter Weed Finder: A Guide to Dry Plants in Winter, Dorcas S. Miller

Fern Finder: A Guide to Native Ferns of Northeastern and Central North America, Anne C. Hallowell

Winter Tree Finder: For Identifying Deciduous Trees in Winter, May Theilgaard Watts and Tom Watts

Plant ID Card Deck:

Wild Cards: Edible Wild Foods, Linda Runyon (U.S. Games Systems, 1990)

Websites

Noxious and Invasive Plants: http://plants.usda.gov/java/noxiousDriver

USDA Fact Sheets & Plant Guides: http://plants.usda.gov/java/factSheet

Wildflowers and Weeds (Thomas J. Elpel / Botany in a Day resources): www.wildflowers-and-weeds.com

PLANT SCIENCE, CULTURE, AND TRADITION

Books

Plain and Happy Living: Amish Recipes and Remedies, Emma Byler (Goosefoot Acres Press, 1991)

Second Nature: A Gardener's Education, Michael Pollan (Dell Publishing, 1991)

The Private Life of Plants: A Natural History of Plant Behaviour, David Attenborough (Princeton University Press [U.S.], Domino Books Ltd. [U.K.], 1995)

Websites

David Attenborough Life and Works: www.bbc.co.uk/nature/programmes/who/david_attenborough.shtml

Michael Pollan Life and Works: www.michaelpollan.com

PUBLIC, PRIVATE, AND SPECIALTY GARDENS

(Check announcements in your area for local garden and estate tours and flower shows during spring and summer.)

Books

Directory of Public Gardens, 9th ed., National Home Gardening Club (2005)

Gardens Across America, Volume I: East of the Mississippi: The American Horticultural Society's Guide to American Public Gardens and Arboreta, John J. Russell (Taylor Trade Publishing, 2005)

Gardens Across America, Volume II: West of the Mississippi: The American Horticultural Society's Guide to American Public Gardens and Arboreta, John J. Russell (Taylor Trade Publishing, 2006)

Guide to Public Gardens, Garden Club of America (1976)

Websites

American Public Gardens Association: www.publicgardens.org or www.aabga.org

European Garden Heritage Network: http://cmsen.eghn.org

Gardenvisit: www.gardenvisit.com/m/garden-finder-indexs/USA.htm

GardenGuides.com U.S. Public Gardens & Garden Walks: www.gardenguides.com/resources/walks/states.asp?c=US

Ketzel Levine's Talking Plants: www.npr.org/programs/talkingplants/features/state

U.S. National Park Service: www.nps.gov

A sampler of U.S. public gardens

Alaska Botanical Garden (Anchorage, Alaska): www.alaskabg.org

Arizona-Sonora Desert Museum (Tucson, AZ): www.desertmuseum.org

(Page for the bloom watch: www.desertmuseum.org/programs/flw_blooming.html)

Atlanta Botanical Garden (Atlanta, GA): www.atlantabotanicalgarden.org

Birmingham Botanical Gardens (Birmingham, AL): www.bbgardens.org

Blithewold Mansion, Gardens, and Arboretum (Bristol, RI):
www.blithewold.org

Brooklyn Botanic Garden (Brooklyn, NY): www.bbg.org

Chicago Botanic Garden (Glencoe, IL): www.chicagobotanic.org

Denver Botanic Gardens (Denver, CO): www.botanicgardens.org/
pageinpage/home.cfm

Desert Botanical Garden (Phoenix, AZ): www.dbg.org

Elizabeth Park (Hartford, CT): www.elizabethpark.org

Fort Worth Botanic Garden (Fort Worth, TX): www.fwbg.org

Hawaii Tropical Botanical Garden (Papaikou, HA):
www.hawaiigarden.com

The Huntington Botanical Gardens (San Marino, California):
www.huntington.org/BotanicalDiv/HEHBotanicalHome.html

Hoyt Arboretum (Portland, Oregon): www.hoytarboretum.org

International Peace Garden (North Dakota-Manitoba border):
www.peacegarden.com

Michigan 4-H Children's Garden (E. Lansing, Michigan):
http://4hgarden.msu.edu/main.html

Missouri Botanical Garden (St. Louis, Missouri): www.mobot.org

Monticello (Thomas Jefferson home) (Charlottesville, Virginia):
www.monticello.org

Mount Auburn Cemetery (Cambridge, Massachusetts):
www.mountauburn.org

San Francisco Botanical Garden (San Francisco, California):
www.sfbotanicalgarden.org

Tyler Municipal Rose Garden (Tyler, Texas):
www.texasrosefestival.com/museum/garden.htm

Wild Gardens of Acadia (Acadia National Park, Maine):
www.acadiamagic.com/wild-gardens.html

A sampler of private garden tours:

Festival of Houses and Gardens (Charleston, South Carolina):
www.historiccharleston.org/news_events/festival.html

Historic Garden Week in Virginia (statewide): www.vagardenweek.org

Secret Garden Tour (Newport, Rhode Island):
www.secretgardentours.org

RAILROAD GARDENING

www.trains.com/TRC/CS/forums/6/ShowForum.aspx (*Garden Railways Magazine* forum)

www.railsusa.com/links/Garden_Railroads

www.gardentrains.com (includes a page for books)

REGIONAL, EXTREME CLIMATE, AND ZONE INFORMATION

Books

Coastal Gardening in the Pacific Northwest: From Northern California to British Columbia, Carla Albright (Taylor Trade Publishing, 2007)

Cold-Climate Gardening: How to Extend Your Growing Season by at Least 30 Days, Lewis Hill (Storey Publishing, 1987)

Dry-Land Gardening: A Xeriscaping Guide for Dry-Summer, Cold-Winter Climates, Jennifer Bennett (Firefly Books, 1998)

Gardening at the Shore, Frances Tenenbaum and Jerry Pavia (Timber Press, 2006)

Gardening in the Tropics, R. E. Holttum and Ivan Enoch (Timber Press, 2005)

Sunbelt Gardening: Success in Hot-Weather Climates, Tom Peace (Fulcrum Publishing, 2000)

Western Garden Book, Kathleen Brenzel and Sunset editors (Sunset Books, 2007)

Xeriscape Handbook: A How-To Guide to Natural, Resource-Wise Gardening, Gayle Weinstein (Fulcrum Publishing, 1999)

Magazines

Carolina Gardener, www.carolinagardener.com/index.php

Chicago Wilderness, http://chicagowildernessmag.org

Garden Compass, www.gardencompass.com

Gardens West, http://gardenswest.com

Georgia Gardening, www.georgiagardening.com

Iowa Gardening, www.iowagardeningmagazine.com

Kansas City Homes and Gardens,
    www.kchomesandgardens.com/kchg/index.html

Long Island Gardening, (no website yet)

Neil Sperry's Gardens: The Definitive Word in Texas Horticulture,
    www.neilsperry.com

San Diego Home/Garden Lifestyles, www.sdhg.net

Subtropical Gardening (Australia), www.stgmagazine.com.au

Sunset Magazine, www.sunset.com/sunset/bookstore/0,20664,2,00.html

Texas Gardener, www.texasgardener.com

The Prairie Garden (Canada), www.theprairiegarden.ca/index.html

Websites

Alpine Gardening:

www.alpinegardensociety.net

www.flower-gardening-made-easy.com/rock-gardening-tips.html

Coastal Gardening:

http://gardeningbythesea.com

www.gulfcoast-gardening.com

Cold-Climate Gardening:

www.hgtv.com/hgtv/gl_seasonal_zones/article/0,,HGTV_3631_216589
    4,00.html

www.northerngardening.com/

www.seedstrust.com/has/highaltitudeseeds.html

www.suite101.com/article.cfm/organic/100507

Desert Gardening:

www.demesne.info/Garden-Help/Desert-Gardening/Desert-Plants.htm

www.ezinearticles.com/?The-Essentials-For-Desert-Landscaping-And-Extreme-Climates&id=660083

www.hgtv.com/hgtv/gl_seasonal_zones/article/0,1785,HGTV_3631_31 56882,00.html

General Regional/Subclimate Gardening:

www.bhg.com/bhg/category.jsp?categoryid=/templatedata/bhg/ category/data/RegionalMonthlyGardenTips.xml

www.weather.com/activities/homeandgarden/garden/education/ gardenawhot.html

Subtropical Gardening:

www.floridaplants.com

www.iloveindia.com/garden/regional-gardening/gardens-humid.html

www.ronsympson.com

Western Gardening:

www.highcountrygardens.com/library

Zone Maps:

www.ahs.org/publications/heat_zone_map.htm

www.raintreenursery.com/map_usdaHardiness.html

www.usna.usda.gov/Hardzone/ushzmap.html

SEED, PLANT, AND SUPPLY CATALOGS

Abundant Life Seeds (OR): www.abundantlifeseeds.com/stores/1/ index.cfm

Bountiful Gardens (CA): www.bountifulgardens.org

Gardener's Supply Company (VT): www.gardeners.com

Gardenocity (FL): www.seedlover.com

Kitchen Garden Seeds (CT): www.kitchengardenseeds.com/about.html

Nourse Farms (MA): www.noursefarms.com

Pinetree Garden Seeds (ME): www.superseeds.com

Richters Herb Specialists (Canada): www.richters.com

Territorial Seed Company (OR): www.territorial-seed.com/stores/1/index.cfm

White Flower Farm (CT): www.whiteflowerfarm.com

SUSTAINABILITY AND ECOLOGY

www.enn.com (Environmental News)

www.solviva.com/index.htm

www.sustainable-gardening.com

www.beyondsustainablegardening.com

www.raingardens.org/Index.php

www.geichina.org

www.monarchwatch.org/waystations

TOPIARY

Books

Illustrated Practical Encyclopedia of Pruning, Training and Topiary: How to Prune and Train Trees, Shrubs, Hedges, Topiary, Tree and Soft Fruit, Climbers and Roses, Richard Bird (Lorenz Books, 2006)

The Book of Topiary, Charles H. Curtis and W. Gibson (Tuttle, 1985)

Topiary: Garden Art in Yew and Box, Nathaniel Lloyd (Garden Art Press, 1999; The Crowood Press, 2006)

Topiary Basics: The Art of Shaping Plants in Gardens & Containers, Margherita Lombardi, C. Serra Zanetti, and John E. Elsley (Sterling, 2001)

Ultimate Topiaries: The Most Magnificent Horticultural Art Through the Years, Elizabeth Buckley (Courage Books, 2004)

Websites

Houseplant topiary: www.lowes.com/lowes/lkn?action=howTo&p=
HomeDecor/Topiary.html

Ladew Gardens ("the most outstanding topiary garden in America"):
www.ladewgardens.com

Railton, Town of Topiary: www.townoftopiary.com.au/topiary.html

Timeless Topiary: www.timelesstopiary.com/about-topiary.php

Topiary Joe: www.topiaryjoe.com

TREES AND FORESTS

American Forests: www.americanforests.org

Big Trees (info and stories): www.mentalfloss.com/blogs/archives/4812

Big Tree Register:
www.americanforests.org/resources/bigtrees/register.php

Vermont Tree Society: www.vermonttreesociety.org/list.htm

URBAN, ROOFTOP, AND COMMUNITY GARDENING

Books

Urban Gardening: A Hong Kong Gardener's Journal, Arthur van Langenberg
(Chinese University Press, 2006)

Websites

American Community Garden Association: www.communitygarden.org

Green Culture in Singapore (information and forum about urban
gardening): www.greenculturesg.com

GreenGrid Roof Systems (commercial, institutional, residential rooftop
gardens): www.greengridroofs.com/projects/index.htm

Guerilla Gardening: www.guerrillagardening.org

New York Restoration Project (Bette Midler): http://nyrp.org

Urban Community Gardens: www.mindspring.com/
~communitygardens

Index

About the Author

Carolyn Haley is a freelance writer and editor doing business as DocuMania. For years she contributed articles to the New England Business Journals, as well as wrote advertorials placed in national magazines such as *Good Housekeeping*, *Redbook*, and *Women's Day*. Her feature article, "The Rural Entertainment Network" (*Bird Watcher's Digest*, Nov./Dec. 2006) recounts her backyard adventures with wildlife at her Vermont home, where she has been opening her heart with gardens for the past decade.

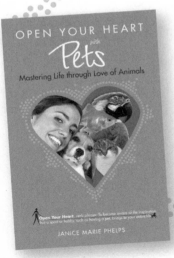